PETTY

Alessandro Roncaglia

PETTY

The Origins
of Political Economy

M. E. SHARPE, INC.
Armonk, New York

A translation of *Petty: la nascita dell'economia politica.*
Italian text copyright © 1977 by Etas Libri S.p.A.

English text © 1985 by M. E. Sharpe, Inc.,
80 Business Park Drive, Armonk, New York 10504

Translated by Isabella Cherubini.

Library of Congress Cataloging in Publication Data

Roncaglia, Alessandro, 1947–
    Petty, the origins of political economy.

    Translation of: Petty.
    Bibliography: p.
    1. Petty, William, Sir, 1623–1687.   2. Economics—History.
3. Classical school of economics—History.   I. Title.
HB103.P5R6613   1985   330.15′3   84-23549
ISBN 0-87332-315-7

Printed in the United States of America

Contents

Introduction

It is now widely accepted that economics is going through a period of crisis. On one side, the logical coherence of traditional marginalist theory, which is embraced by the majority of academic economists, is being questioned by the evermore fundamental criticisms of its solution to the problems of value and distribution. On the other side, Marxian theory has not yet been able to provide acceptable solutions to the problems that its founder left unresolved.

Confronted with such a situation, the study of the ideas of an author who wrote in the seventeenth century might appear as a futile flight from the reality of today's problems to seek refuge in antiquity. But it should be recognized that such a judgment is based on a mistaken distinction between economic theory and the history of economic thought, mistaken, because it is linked to the Schumpeterian idea of a linear development of economic theory, understood in the restrictive sense of a box of tools for use in analysis. In the wider sense of "vision" (*Weltanschauung*), as Schumpeter himself recognized, political economy does not follow a straight, cumulative path of development. At the very least, in some very important respects, the return or rediscovery of conceptions that have previously been considered as outmoded is not only possible, but has regularly occurred. The vision or conception of the world adopted by each school or group of economists in fact determines the choice of the problems that are considered as most relevant and the framework in which their analysis is attempted. In this sense the "vision" adopted implies the very instruments of analysis. As a consequence, it is only possible to discover a linear path of development of economic theory within each particular "vision of the world," which then serves as a criterion for the judgment of ideas that are external to that system of thought.

In other words, there is a particular reconstruction of the history of economic thought corresponding to each theoretical school: from Clas-

Thanks to F. Donzelli, M. Salvati, M. Tonveronachi, and G. Vaggi for useful comments and suggestions on a first draft of this essay.

sical or liberal historicism, the most illustrious example of which is to be found in Book IV of Smith's *Wealth of Nations*, to the Marxian position represented in *The Theories of Surplus Value*, then to the Schumpeterian and marginalist interpretations, and finally to the more recent attempts (such as Dobb's *Theories of Value and Distribution since Adam Smith*) to extend Marxian historicism by explicitly taking into account the contribution of Sraffa's theory of prices.

Now, only by adopting an extremely restrictive conception could the ultimate objective of the history of economic thought be considered as the simple reconstruction of the gradual revision and improvement of the analysis developed by each particular line of thought, culminating with its most recent formulation. The strictly analytical debates between the various opposing schools which frequently occur may often appear to be examples of a discussion of the deaf if one does not keep clearly in mind that the discussions generally go far beyond specific problems of analysis to questions of the entire frame of reference, conceptual and methodological, most relevant in economic analysis. Historical investigation can expand our knowledge of such differences in the frames of reference of different schools, analyzing the origins and the evolution of the various concepts employed.

Our study of Petty's contribution should be understood within this context, and the limitations of such an approach recognized (we will not, for example, consider Petty as a demographer or geographer, and even in terms of his more strictly economic work, the weight attributed to his various contributions may differ from that which he gave them in his written works). There are a number of desirable aspects associated with the point of reference provided by this approach which, in our opinion, can be of use to the theoretical economist. As Petty himself observed with reference to Ireland, the analysis of a mode of production in its initial stage of development, when it has not yet had time to develop its complete structure, can provide a useful aid to an understanding of the fully developed mode of production. Thus the study of the birth of fundamental economic concepts and of the interrelationships that originally existed among them may prove useful in improving our understanding of basic economic categories, of their possible significance, and of their multiple reciprocal interrelationships. In this context, William Petty occupies a position of particular importance for two reasons: the epoch in which he lived and his position within the pre-Marxian history of economic thought.

The epoch in which Petty lived was one of primary accumulation, of the birth of capitalism. Petty's participation in the events of this period (in particular the division of Irish land) and the close relationship of his writings to those events, allows us to grasp the interrelationships between the development of certain theoretical concepts and the parallel development of the corresponding elements constituting the reality of the capitalist economic system. And Petty, as Marx was the first to recognize, had a decisive role in adapting the categories already in existence at the birth of the mode of production, such as those of natural law and price, and in creating new ones. All this, while it helps to understand the character of political economy, considered as an interpretation of capitalism, as a historically determined science, also explains how Marx could consider Petty as the "founder of political economy."

Naturally, Petty's work was particularly influenced by the period in which he lived. For this reason it seems opportune to start our examination of Petty's economic contributions with a brief sketch of his life and times, to try to situate this lively thinker in the proper historical context. Chapter 1 is dedicated to this task. Among other things, as we shall see more clearly in that chapter, the conditions of Petty's "active life" were more essential and predominant with respect to his "contemplative life." It is the first which provides the stimulus and the material for the ratiocination of the second. Such reflection, even when it is represented as a simple refuge from the disappointments of reality, is in fact always an instrument linked to the development of new positions of action. In the initial phases of capitalist development, that of primary accumulation, Petty's personal adventures render him an emblematic figure. From a number of viewpoints his ideas present a faithful reflection of his position as a member of the nascent class of capitalists then developing on the basis of appropriation of the means of production, primarily of land. Petty is an exemplary expression and representation of the historical role of that class in the development of the productive forces by means of reorganization of the productive system.

After this introduction to Petty's life and works, the following chapters will present an analysis of the various aspects of the contribution of the English economist. In chapter 2, dedicated to the problems of methodology, we will encounter the idea of "political arithmetic," of which Petty is the recognized founder. Investigation of the meaning and intention behind this idea shows that it cannot be considered as the simple introduction of some fundamental considerations of statistical methodology into economic research. We shall discover instead that it is connected to Baconian epistomology and to Petty's adoption of an objective viewpoint which, as we will try to show in the succeeding chapter, is clearly reflected in his conception of the problem of value. The examination of the methodological problem thus allows us to trace out a scheme of analysis which will be followed in the subsequent chapters whose contents will be only briefly reviewed here.

To prepare the way for more complex problems such as the analysis of the concept of an economic system and the framework given to the problem of value and prices (which will constitute the subjects of chapters 6, 7, and 8) we will first undertake a preliminary examination of some particular aspects of Petty's analysis, such as money (chapter 3), international trade (chapter 4), and the fiscal system (chapter 5). Among other things, the analysis in these chapters is necessary in order to furnish a sufficiently clear idea of the range of Petty's economic ideas. It should not be necessary to warn the reader that the analysis is carried out without any pretension of producing a complete, logical coherent general system of analysis of the economy. As Hull, the editor of Petty's economic writings, rightly stresses, it would be dangerous to attempt to reconstruct a full-fledged "treatise" by combining the various hints and ideas scattered here and there in his several works which were originally written with precise practical goals in mind. It is Adam Smith who initiated the tradition of the great treatise, considered to be a systematic and complete treatment of the subject, at least in the opinion of its author. As a consequence of the rudimentary development of Petty's theoretical apparatus, the examination of subjects such as money, the fiscal system, and international trade can be undertaken without having first developed Petty's position on the problems of value and prices, which in reality constitute the central core of economic theory and would thus normally represent the logical premise for the analysis of such particular problems. This fact permits the identification of the methodological and conceptual framework in which Petty carries out his analysis of prices and of value before setting out the detailed examination of Petty's ideas in this area.

For the same reasons it will be possible to carry out an examination of the concept of an economic system and of some elements of the theory of growth and development (in chapter 6), of the concept of the surplus and of the sparse indications of a theory of distribution (in chapter 7), and of the relations between normal and current prices (in chapter 8), before arriving, in the same chapter, at the problem of the theory of value and distribution. In this regard we will attempt to demonstrate that Petty is not simply a precursor of Marx's labor theory of value, but something more as well as something different. It would, indeed, appear more correct in Petty's case to speak of a theory of land-

and-labor value or, more precisely, of a physical-cost theory of value. Even if Petty is far from providing a definitive solution of the problem of value and of prices, the manner in which he framed the problem, with direct reference to "physical costs," made it possible for his analysis to provide, as has already been pointed out, a useful reference point for the understanding of contemporary economic debate.

The conclusions of this essay will be provisional and partial. In effect, this book is not intended to be anything more than a useful introduction. Useful, on the one hand, as an introduction to the study of the theory of prices in its most modern form, because it helps us to understand the configuration of the productive system (with the various associated problems from the concept of the state to the fiscal system, from population to money) in which the problem of prices is framed. Useful, on the other side, as an introduction to the study of the theory of value, because it helps us to identify those concepts that are basic and necessary to the formulation of an "objective" theory of value. This double direction suggested by the analysis of Petty's ideas indicates that their further study should be particularly fruitful to an understanding of modern economic analysis.

Perugia, October 1976

Note to this Edition

Only a few changes have been introduced in the preparation of this translation of the Italian text. In this regard thanks are due for useful comments and suggestions to P. Groenewegen, and especially to J. A. Kregel. In the period since the original publication of this book, only one really relevant paper dealing with Petty's work (Matsukawa, 1977) has come to my attention. References to this paper have been introduced at the appropriate places in the text below.

Rome, November 1983

1

William Petty:
His Life and Works

1.1 William Petty was born May 26, 1623, the twentieth year of the reign of James I, in the village of Romsey, Hampshire.[1] He was the third of six children born into the family of a clothier, and the eldest of three who survived childhood illness. At the age of thirteen, after a minimal education at his village school, which included a bit of Latin, he set out as a cabin boy on a merchant ship plying the coasts of England and France. In an accident ten months later he broke his leg and was put ashore on the French coast, passing his convalescence in Caen. He supported himself there by giving Latin and English lessons, and also managed to earn some money on small trading ventures. It was his ability to express himself in Latin that eventually gained Petty admission to the local Jesuit college where he studied Latin, Greek, French, mathematics, and astronomy. On his return to England he entered the Royal Navy, but in 1643, at the age of twenty, he abandoned his homeland for the Netherlands, where he joined numerous other refugees from the civil war between King and Parliament. His interest turned to medicine, which he studied in Utrecht, Leiden and Amsterdam. By 1645 he had moved on to Paris where he specialized in anatomy with Hobbes (who was the same age as Petty's father).

He also made the acquaintance of the many scholars who had gathered around Father Mersen and the Marquis of Newcastle, and of various other refugees from the civil war. On his return to Romsey in 1646, Petty became involved in the running of his father's business affairs (his father had died in 1644), although he clearly never gave up the idea of returning to the rather more exciting world of intellectual discourse which he had come to know during his travels. Indeed, only a year later traces of him can be found in London where he engaged in an unsuccessful attempt to exploit a personal invention, a machine capable of producing two copies of a written text simultaneously, for which he obtained a patent in 1647.[2]

In 1648 Petty arrived in Oxford, where he quickly completed his medical studies and was awarded the degree of doctor of medicine. In rapid succession he was elected Fellow of Brasenose College and then its Vice-Principal. Starting his academic career as deputy to Clayton, the Professor of Anatomy, he then quickly succeeded him, in January 1650, at the age of twenty-seven. In addition to support from Clayton, who seems to have rather disliked dissecting cadavers and was pleased to resign such tasks to his more than able deputy, Petty's phenomenal advance was also favored by the political unrest of the period. Cromwell's victory over the King led to an antiroyalist housecleaning of the intellectual circles of the University, leaving room for the rapid advancement of those who possessed some personal political influence and the support of well-placed friends. Petty, moreover, was more than willing to use any and every occasion to exploit his own fame and fortune, to which the episode of Ann Green amply testifies. In December 1650 a young girl who had been found guilty of infanticide was hanged. She had, however, managed to survive hanging and Petty not only revived her on the dissecting table, but succeeded in nursing her back to health. Soon afterwards an anonymous pamphlet appeared, sensationally entitled *News from the Dead* and complete with florid English and Latin verse (possibly written in part by Petty himself), extolling Petty's miraculous medical feat in defiance of death and the hangman.

Clearly Petty could have enjoyed a brilliant medical career.[3] Indeed, he himself mentioned this towards the end of his life fain to express regret that he most certainly did not feel, yet medicine was destined to be but another of the many episodes in his continuous endeavor to achieve fame and fortune. In 1651 he transferred from the Chair of Anatomy at Oxford to the Chair of Music at Gresham College London,[4] largely on the support of his friends and in particular of Captain John Graunt, who was to exercise an important influence on Petty throughout his life. A short time later Petty again left England (although he managed to conserve his existing appointments and emoluments), this time for Ireland as the chief medical officer of the English army sent to the island to quell the Catholic rebels and as personal physician to the Lieutenant General and his family, General Lambert, and General Fleetwood. While in Ireland Petty finally abandoned permanently the practice of medicine, and dedicated himself to the intellectual pursuits and business activities that were indeed to make him rich and famous.

1.2 Petty arrived in Ireland in 1652, when Cromwell's armies had already put down the Irish rebellion. In ten years of fighting, according to Petty's own calculations, 616,000 men, women, and children had been killed out of a population of 1,466,000 persons at the beginning of the rebellion in 1641.[5] The count, however, included not only the victims felled in battle and the masses of innocents put to the sword, but also the victims of the famine which was the inevitable consequence of a war fought on a territory as poor as Ireland. With the ancient feudal institutions uprooted and the previously existing distribution of land destroyed by force of arms, Ireland presented itself as an enormous *tabula rasa* upon which a gigantic experiment in primitive accumulation might be carried out. Nearly all of Ireland was now "free" to be distributed to new owners, substituting the relations of private property for the ancient feudal relations between lord and serf which had existed in many parts of the island.

The forfeited lands were contested by a number of different interest groups. First claim was held by the "Adventurers" (in name and in deed), a group of well-off English bankers and landlords who had advanced the monies necessary to finance the expeditionary forces to Ireland. The repayments specified in the loan contracts were on the basis of the forfeited holdings of the Catholic rebels. Next came the officers and soldiers of the invading armies who were owed substantial amounts in back pay. They were closely followed by the old English settlers who had been expropriated by the Catholics in the early stages of the war. Of course, the English treasury had been depleted by the lengthy conflict and required replenishment. Finally, an entire county, Connaught, was to be reserved as an immense concentration camp for all the Irish who had been driven from their original places of residence by armed conflict or expropriation.

It was not long before a debate broke out over the problem of the "transplantation," i.e., the forced physical transfer of the remnant Irish population to county Connaught. In 1655 Petty and Sir Vincent Gookin, member of Parliament and of the Privy Council (which at that time had the function of the modern Cabinet), together wrote an anonymously published pamphlet with the self-explanatory title *A Discourse against the Transplantation into Connaught*. The reasons for their opposition, as set out in the pamphlet, were far from humanitarian.[6] Rather, they were more concerned that the concentration of the English and Irish populations in two separate and distinct regions of the country, much as in two opposing army camps, would be the source of permanent tension and conflict between them. In addition, they noted that the confinement of the indigent population in one county would deprive the English settlers of their source of cheap labor, with unfortunate consequences on the value of their landed property. However, reports of the massacre in 1654 of Protestants in the Oise Valley with the active participation of Irish soldiers in exile on the continent and at the order of Duke Carl Emmanuel II of Savoy, under pressure from the Jesuits, made the conciliatory position of Petty and Gookin politically untenable, and the division of Ireland and the transplantation of the population went ahead according to the original plan.

Obviously, the division of land among the various competing groups, as well as among the individual components of the particular groups, presented enormous practical difficulties. It was necessary to survey several million acres, and to subdivide them into thousands of allotments of various sizes corresponding to the credits claimed by each individual, taking into consideration the differing value of the land due to differences in geographical location and the relative fertility of each allotment. Such a complicated task could not be carried out to each participant's satisfaction, nor could it be completed without attempts at subversion, corruption, or outright bribery. Even a perfect division would have been accompanied by skepticism and suspicion. The task of carrying out the division was initially assigned to Benjamin Worsley, who was given the title of "Surveyor General." His first decision was to carry out what was called the "Grosse Survey," an enumeration of the confiscated territories with brief descriptive notes on each entry. This list was to serve as the basis for the initial calculations to determine the division of the counties among the various competing groups of creditor-aspirant proprietors. Few general maps of the area were available to accompany the verbal descriptions and the work of enumeration, initiated in August 1653, was extremely slow. In addition, the prospective cost of the operation was high, and the extremely general and rough nature of the evaluation and distribution engendered considerable discontent, especially among the soldiers who were awaiting its completion before their discharge.

It was in these conditions that Petty came forward, initially with a series of criticisms and suggestions to Worsley, who rejected them outright and in 1654 proceeded to an initial distribution of land to the most vocal and active of the malcontents. This only served to renew the debate over the Survey and Petty took advantage of the general state of discontentment to directly attack the projected "Civil Survey" which was to follow the "Grosse Survey." He put forward his own proposal for a "Down Survey," to be based on a topographical survey leading to the drafting of detailed maps, instead of the simple lists of lands whose subsequent identity was often subject to dispute.[7] As might be expected, discussions of the competing projects were accompanied by multiple intrigues and maneuvers by both Worsley and Petty. Although Petty's proposal was accepted, it would not be correct to say that he was triumphant. While Petty was given the awesome responsibility, in December 1654, for the execution of a topographical survey to define the land destined for the English soldiers, and also for the construction of general maps of Ireland, Worsley retained his official position as Surveyor General as well as the right to oversee the progress of the work and to judge its acceptability relative to the conditions stipulated in the official contract.

In completing the survey project within the fixed terms Petty demonstrated remarkable abilities. His sustained personal commitment, in addition to his highly developed organizational ability meant that the highly complex operation was completed without delay, despite the enormous difficulties presented by the inclement weather which transformed vast areas of land into swamps, and by the bands of rebel Irishmen who persistently attacked the squads of men charged with the survey which would be used to distribute ''their'' lands to the conquering foreigner. Petty's remarkable abilities were concretely expressed in two factors: the adoption of a complex system of division of labor and the use of common soldiers for the work of actual measurement. This sharply reduced the amount of work to be done by qualified surveyors and thus the number of them required. In addition, to assure consistent supplies, small units were set up to produce the required surveying equipment. Division of labor was also prescribed for the draftsmen charged with translating the results into maps.[8] The use of ordinary soldiers, who were accustomed to heavy work in inclement weather and to traversing rough terrain, and who were directly interested in the successful completion of the project, produced a willing and effective work force. In all, more than a thousand people were occupied by the project. In the autumn of 1656 the survey was completed and the division of the land among the interested parties commenced. Even so, when Petty attempted to claim payment and the recovery of his surety bond, the completion was challenged and payment was delayed for two years. Petty still managed to be the most active member of the committee charged with the distribution of the lands to the English soldiers. He was also, together with his rival Worsley, supervisor of the survey of the land destined for the ''Adventurers'' and later, in 1658, a member of the committee responsible for overseeing and distribution. Indeed, it was in this last phase that he succeeded in obtaining for himself the greatest pecuniary benefit, largely as a result of his business acumen and his ability to manipulate governmental bureaucracy, qualities he commanded in the same measure as his organizational talent. Always decrying the injustices that were continually being committed against him (in this he was not dissimilar from anyone else directly interested in the distribution), and without directly violating any of the regulations that bound him, Petty emerged from the affair with a large monetary recompense and, most important, a landed estate with parcels in every Irish county, but in particular in County Kerry.[9] To accomplish this Petty availed himself of the active trade in debentures, i.e., the right to land which many recipients—especially, the common soldiers—were forced to sell in order to raise the small sums of ready cash for their necessary maintenance. In his purchases Petty put his direct knowledge of the methods used in the surveys to good use. He thus succeeded in procuring for himself large parcels of ground officially classified as "unproductive" and thus unwanted, although the land had other potential profitable uses.

1.3 Petty carried out his work in a rapidly evolving institutional context, and political factors exercised a determining influence on his activities. No legal contract or political decision could be considered as definitively decided or closed; this was particularly true in respect to the rights to landed property, which were continually open to challenge. It was in this context that Petty proposed that an Irish Land Registry should be set up (on the model of the *Kadaster* already in existence in the Netherlands[10]) in order to provide stability and security to those who had been awarded rights to Irish landed property. He argued that the expenses of the Registry, which were to be met by the new landowners, would be insignificant compared with the legal fees they would be compelled to pay in order to defend their legally conferred rights to the land against continual challenge. There was, of course, a certain personal interest in the proposal, and Petty was well known as someone who actively defended what he considered to be his legitimate interests.

From the completion of the Down Survey to the time of his death Petty was in fact involved, irrespective of his own volition, in an incredible number of litigations, interspersed with a long series of petitions to the highest political authorities on his own behalf. Even though Petty continually protested that he was unjustly treated, he seems to have emerged victorious in most, if not all, of the litigations in which he was involved. He managed to avoid paying the major part of the taxes (from his point of view excessive) that the assessors had levied on his landholdings, and he was exonerated of charges of acting for his private interest while in public office, corruption, abuse of power in public office, and of other charges of the sort at a time when such activities were common and, as far as one can tell, were generally practiced by even the most indignant of Petty's accusers.

His legal battles were also accompanied by other similarly occasioned adventures, such as a challenge to a duel, arrest for contempt of court (which lasted only a few days), and a physical attack by a rival which left Petty with a disabled eye. In his encounters with his adversaries Petty employed what was a two-edged weapon—his caustic repartee—which his contemporaries considered to be without equal. Although his biting remarks were always to the point, Petty's inability to temper his comments in delicate circumstances frequently caused embarrassment and was often the occasion of permanent ill feeling.

Petty's financial and political position, like that of many other newly created landowners in Ireland, was made particularly precarious by the Restoration of 1660.[11] The adoption of a policy of increased tolerance of Catholics caused renewed discussion on the division of the conquered Irish lands among the English victors. Despite the repeated promises of Charles and the decrees that made the existing situation binding on the new government (the Act of Settlement, 1662, and the Act of Explanation, 1665, which explicitly guaranteed to Petty, by name, the right to most of his holdings), Irish Catholics successfully challenged several of the acts of confiscation decreed in the Cromwellian period. Petty's holdings seem to have been well protected by Royal Letter and then by the Acts. Yet the Court of Innocents, which was instituted after the Restoration to decide on these questions, did show a marked partiality to the Catholic claims. Petty did not fail to point this out, citing as examples episodes of false testimony and the existence of a "Catholic Block" ready to commit any illegal act in order to recover land held by the "English Block."[12]

However, the bureaucratic formalities of the Court meant that only a small proportion of the cases that were brought could actually be heard, and this fact Petty avoided mentioning.

Petty thus found it necessary to travel frequently between England and Ireland,[13] on the one hand to cultivate the political contacts necessary for the successful outcome of his legal proceedings, and on the other to follow the cases personally and to oversee the administration of his estates.

Among other improvements, around 1670 he established iron and copper works as well as a fishing industry on his holdings in County Kerry, which were designed to be vertically integrated from the mine to the blast furnace in the first case, and from the sewing of the fishing nets to the building and operation of the boats in the second.

1.4 In 1659 Petty returned to London, where he had acquired a large parcel of land. The construction of the buildings he had projected for that area was interrupted by the fire that destroyed a large part of the city in 1666. His renewed residence in London afforded Petty the opportunity to resume contact with English friends, in particular with the group who, like himself, had been members of the Philosophical Society at Oxford and now met periodically at Gresham College. On November 28, 1660, the group decided to form a permanent association which would meet regularly under the guidance of established rules and regulations. Two years later, on July 25, 1662, the association received Royal Approval as the Royal Society for the Improving of Natural Knowledge.

The minutes of the Society indicate that Petty played an important role in its constitution and took a lively interest in its activities. His primary intellectual interest, in addition to the political arithmetic to which he owes his fame, appears to have been naval engineering. When his plans for a double-bottomed ship (a sort of catamaran) met with general skepticism, he did not hestitate to finance the construction of a series of prototypes with his own funds. After a brief initial success, the trials produced a series of irremediable failures.

The orientation of the Royal Society was rigorously positivist: theory should be based on fact and supported by verifiable data or, when possible, with experiments carried out in the presence of other members. Petty went so far as to propose, in jest, that the annual meetings of the Society should be on the feast day of Saint Thomas, to honor the apostle who believed only in what he could see or touch.[14] The principles of the Royal Society, which were subsequently to become the basis of the predominant research criteria in the natural sciences, at the time constituted the credo of a distinct minority of cultured gentlemen, and of an even smaller number in the academic world. Both the Royal Society and Gresham College were institutions that reflected the cultural revolution which accompanied the birth of capitalism in England. This position in the avant-garde may explain a certain bias in approach and purity of principle; yet it is difficult to overestimate the importance of this group of men and their activities. The institutions they created were to focus attention on problems that were of more or less direct interest to the world of industrial production (astronomy for navigation, which would facilitate international trade, chemistry and physics, mathematics and bookkeeping, and engineering)[15] in place of the metaphysical problems which had preoccupied science in the Middle Ages.

It was in this cultural atmosphere that Petty founded his new science of Political Arithmetick. Later chapters will examine Petty's methodology and the content of his scientific work. For present purposes it is sufficient to underline that the intellectual current in which these works were created and to which they were directed is evident in two essential features: the works were based on the gathering and interpreting of objective data and were conceived for practical ends—the constitution of a science of good government. It was not, for example, for simple intellectual diversion that Petty undertook his investigations of the wealth of England, but rather as a necessary part of his investigation into an improved foreign policy, and as a basis for an improved system of taxation. "Understanding for action," a formula that was later proposed by Marx,[16] seems to correspond closely to the cultural practice of the emerging ruling classes.

Although Petty was a prolific writer, he was little interested in divulging his work to the general public and he frequently refused formal publication.[17] Of his published writings a number were published anonymously, and in one case there is a good probability that Petty was, if not the author, the major contributor to a work that appeared under the name of a friend: *Natural and Political Observations on the Bills of Mortality*, published in London in 1622 under the name of John Graunt, a work of fundamental importance for the history of ideas in the field of statistics and demography.[18] This behavior can be explained in part by the fact that Petty himself considered his research and writing as an escape, a refuge from the reality of the sharply contested battles in which he was forced to engage in order to augment and also defend his wealth and position.[19] It is also true, however, that his behavior was influenced by the fact that his works were addressed to a restricted circle of friends and influential acquaintances, and in some cases to the King directly; and it is not impossible that he also feared negative reactions from the less enlightened general public. It would thus be far from correct to deduce that his actions were those of a dispassionate and disinterested observer of public events, rather than calculated attempts to influence events. For example, while some of Petty's works demonstrating the strength of the English economy were made available to the general public, others written for the same purpose were restricted to private circulation, because the direct comparisons Petty drew in them between the conditions in France and in England might have offended the powerful allies of the English sovereign. It was necessary that such works be restricted to the King

and the most influential advisors in his entourage for they were intended to bring about changes in the direction of English foreign policy.
Other statistical calculations and proposals for reform,[20] though made
available to influential members of the court, were not made public,
probably to avoid creating the impression that conditions could have
been much better than they were had it not been for the incompetence of
the government. Following the example of his illustrious teacher
Hobbes, Petty always demonstrated the highest respect for the authority of the State and tended to identify with the restricted group of men in
power, even though he never succeeded in obtaining high office and,
after the Down Survey, was never again to assume important political
or administrative responsibilities. At the same time, he exhibited a
marked skepticism concerning the capacity of the governed (even when
they were of the wealthiest class) to influence the decisions of the
government. Therefore he chose the direct approach in his attempts to
convince the men who governed of the correctness of his ideas rather
than the indirect route of appeal to the general public and from there to
the government. All things considered, it is apparent that Petty's activity as an economist, far from being a simple diversion from weightier
problems, was an integral part of his political and business activity.

1.5 Petty did seem to regard the realm of personal relationships as
being subordinate to his other activities, or at least that is the impression that is given by his nontechnical writings and personal letters. He
seemed to consider that his main task as a good *pater familias* was to
provide for the material well-being of his family. For example, as his
papers testify, it is only in his later years that he took any interest in the
education of his children.[21] Petty had married rather late in life, at the
age of 44, and had fathered at least one illegitimate child. Neither was
his wife in the blush of youth. Elizabeth Waller had been a widow with
two children. Contemporaries described her as good-looking and intel-
ligent. She was something of a contrast to Petty, accustomed as he was
from childhood to simple pleasures and hard work, for she had a light
and humorous character and enjoyed luxury. Yet, she was Petty's equal
in her ability to administer the family's fortunes, as her inspections of
their Irish estates during his frequent absences in London (due to illness
and problems in Court) amply demonstrate.

The couple had five children. The first two died in infancy in 1670,
to the extreme distress of their mother, although the father, even if
disappointed seemed to consider such occurrences as being in the
nature of things[22] (indeed, Petty's writings assume a 50% infant mor-

tality rate for good times in the absence of epidemics). The surviving children, Anne, born in 1672, Charles, 1673, and Henry, 1675, all outlived their parents.

Family life was marked by continual travel between Ireland and England, for although Petty most frequently traveled alone, it was normal for his wife, and often the entire family, to follow after him. As government policy evolved in favor of rapprochement with the Catholics, the time required to defend Petty's Irish landholdings continually increased. Conditions were exacerbated when James II, a Catholic, succeeded Charles II to the throne in February 1685. Petty had previous acquaintance with the new King, who as Duke of York had been Lord of the Admiralty and had been involved, although demonstrating great skepticism, in Petty's attempt to perfect the double-bottomed ship. Thus in 1685 Petty once again moved his principal residence from Dublin to London,[23] where he succeeded in establishing good relations with the new sovereign. He was frequently received at Court to explain personally to the King the results of his political arithmetic and to describe his numerous suggestions for revisions of the fiscal system and other arguments.[24] None of these proposals were favorably received, however, and Petty did not benefit from any royal intercessions in his legal contests.

In his advanced years, nearly blind and afflicted by what appears to have been a form of gout, Petty was reduced to dictating to secretaries his never-ending stream of scientific and political works, and was unable to revise or correct them. He was also in frequent correspondence with his wife's cousin, Sir Robert Southwell, who had resigned his offices and retired to the country on the accession of James II. Southwell continually cautioned Petty to be prudent in his Irish dealings, urging him, among other things, to abandon the numerous court cases still pending which Petty had brought in defense of his property rights. The other favorite argument of the correspondence concerns the education of his children. Until his death Petty assiduously attended the meetings of the Royal Society. He was among the few who enthusiastically received the publication of Newton's *Principia*, and he complained of his inability to study the diagrams.[25] Indeed, it was at an annual banquet of the Royal Society that he had a relapse and a few days later, on December 26, 1687, he died. His body is interred in a sarcophagus in Romsey Abbey in the village of his birth.

1.6 Only a small part of Petty's written work was published during his lifetime under his own name. Due to the change in political climate more favorable to his ideas, brought about by the "glorious revolution" of 1688, a number of other works were published soon after his death. Between 1895 and 1928 further material came to light and the editor of the last items to appear, Lord Lansdowne (a direct descendant of Petty), notes that the family is still in possession of a good deal of unpublished material, although it is of little interest, principally relating to Petty's business affairs and family matters, numerous letters written in Latin, various licentious satires, a long autobiography, and essays on medicine and naval engineering.

Petty's first published works do not concern economic problems. They comprise a leaflet and a pamphlet issued in 1648 to advertise his first invention, the machine which was to enable the writer to make more copies of a work simultaneously. In the same year another pamphlet, *The Advice of W.P. to Mr Samuel Hartlib for the Advancement of Some Particular Parts of Learning*, appeared outlining projects for the diffusion of the sciences and the technical arts and, a short time later, two works dealing with his private Irish problems: *A Brief of Proceedings between Sir Hierom Sankey and Dr. William Petty* (1659) and *Reflections upon Some Persons and Things in Ireland by Letters to and from Dr. Petty* (1660). In 1662 the *Natural and Political Observations upon the Bills of Mortality*, generally attributed to John Graunt, but which Petty is certain to have authored at least in part, appeared. In that same year the anonymous *A Treatise of Taxes and Contributions* appeared in the first of three printings (1667, 1679, and 1685, the second unauthorized). In 1667 the *History of the Royal Society of London*, edited by T. Sprat, contained a short contribution by Petty on the history of the methods used to dye cloth. In 1674 the Royal Society acted as publisher for *The Discourse Concerning the Use of Duplicate Proportion. Colloquium Davidis cum anima sua* (a paraphrase of the 104th Psalm), written during Petty's short incarceration for contempt of court, was published three years afterward in 1679, anonymously. Two of Petty's economic-statistical writings appeared somewhat later in 1683, *Observations upon the Dublin-Bills of Mortality* and *Another Essay in Political Arithmetic, Concerning the Growth of the City of London*. The *Philosophical Transactions* of the next two years contain brief contributions on land transport, the analysis of mineral waters, and comments on the list of experiments proposed by the Dublin Society, the Irish counterpart of the Royal Society. In 1686 came publication of *An Essay Concerning the Multiplication of Mankind*, the French version of *Two Essays on Political Arithmetick, Concerning the People, Housing, Hospitals, etc. of London and Paris* (published in English the following year), then in the *Philosophical Transactions* a short reply to some critics of his previous publications, and finally *Further Observations upon the Dublin-bills*. In the last year of his life, 1687, Petty published his *Observations upon the Cities of London and Rome* and *Five Essays in Political Arithmetick*.

Shortly after his death, with the rise to power of William of Orange, some of Petty's most important works were finally published. Many of them had enjoyed wide circulation among his friends and at Court and in the Royal Society, and numerous manuscript copies had been made of them. The *Political Arithmetick*, written in 1676, was published officially in 1690 with the 1664 *Verbum Sapienti* as an Appendix. The 1672 *Political Anatomy of Ireland* appeared in 1691 and the 1682 *Quantulumcumque Concerning Money* was published in 1695. By 1683 a pirate edition of *Political Arithmetick* had been issued under the title *The Fourth Part of the Present State of England*.

A large number of Petty's noneconomic writings were published posthumously, among the most important the *History of the Cromwellian Survey of Ireland* and the *Hiberniae Delineatio* (which contains the maps that Petty had prepared on the basis of the Down Survey). Neither work shows a date of publication.

Some additional economic writings had to wait for the Hull edition of Petty's economic works[26] (which included *A Treatise of Ireland*, 1687 and *The Dialogue of Diamonds*) or the Marquis of Lansdowne's editions of unpublished works and correspondence between Petty and Sir Robert Southwell. It is to these later editions of Petty's works, and in particular to the Hull collection, that modern students of Petty most often refer.

The collection of Petty's economic writings edited by the American scholar Charles H. Hull appeared in two volumes in 1899 under the title *The Economic Writings of Sir William Petty*. The first volume contains, in addition to a detailed and highly interesting introduction[27] by Hull himself (which gives major emphasis to the statistical-demographic aspects of Petty's work as against the more strictly theoretical, e.g., the theory of prices and the theory of value), *A Treatise of Taxes and Contributions*, *Verbum Sapienti*, *The Political Anatomy of Ireland* and the *Political Arithmetick*. The second volume contains the *Quantulumcumque Concerning Money*, various essays on political arithmetic and the various *Observations* (among which is the *Natural and Political Observations upon the Bills of Mortality* commonly attributed to Graunt), *A Treatise of Ireland*, selected passages from the *Discourse of Duplicate Proportion* and *The Dialogue of Diamonds*, as well as a bibliographical appendix.

Henry Fitzmaurice, the sixth Marquis of Lansdowne and a direct descendant of Petty (great great grandson of Petty's daughter), published in 1927 a two-volume collection of various manuscripts that had been in the family's possession: *The Petty Papers, Some Unpublished Writings of Sir William Petty, edited from the Bowood Papers*.[28] The subjects of this collection range from political and economic to philosophical and religious, from an outline for a dictionary to questions of military technology, from problems of the colonization of America to English and Latin verse.

The same diversity of interests can be found in *The Petty-Southwell Correspondence, 1676–1687*, also edited by the Marquis of Lansdowne.[29] Both the *Correspondence* and *The Petty Papers* are vital to a complete understanding of Petty as a person and of the various aspects of his intellectual character. From the purely economic point of view, however, they only serve to confirm what can already be clearly deduced on the basis of the writings contained in the *Economic Writings* edited by Hull, or possibly to clarify points of minor detail.

Petty's basic works have been translated into several languages. *The Treatise of Taxes and Contributions, The Political Anatomy of Ireland* and the *Quantulumcumque Concerning Money* have been translated into Italian, edited by F. Colussi with a preface by P. Dockes.[30] The Hull editions of *Economic Writings* have been translated into French by H. Dussauze with a preface by A. Schatz in place of Hull's original introduction.[31]

A complete bibliography of the English editions of Petty's works has been published by Geoffrey Keynes,[32] brother of the better known John Maynard. Hull appended a detailed, but not complete, bibliography to his edition of the *Economic Writings*. From the list of reprints it is clear that Petty's work has never been completely forgotten, although it has never been considered required reading for students of economics. Neither Smith nor Ricardo cites any of Petty's works, and although McCulloch includes *Quantulumcumque Concerning Money* in one of the two volumes of pre-Smithian economic writings that he edited[33] for the Political Economy Club, the very title of the volume, *A Select Collection of Scarce and Valuable Tracts on Money*, as well as its limited circulation of 125 copies reserved for members of the Club, are an indication of the popularity that Petty enjoyed among post-Smithian economists.

The rediscovery of the founder of Political Arithmetick at the end of the nineteenth century is probably explained by the efforts made to this end by his descendants, in conjunction with the reevaluation of Petty's work by Marx, who cited Petty numerous times in his writings. In 1894 a long study, originally a doctoral thesis, by W.L. Bevan appeared with the title *Sir William Petty: A Study in English Economic Literature*.[34] In addition to a summary of all the then available information on Petty, ample quotations giving Petty's position on some of the principal questions in economic theory were given. Bevan's work is assessed and critized in book reviews by H. Higgs[35] and Hull.[36]

Of much greater import, such that it remains today the essential source on the subject, is Petty's biography by his descendant Edmond G. P. Fitzmaurice,[37] which also contains Petty's Last Will and Testament, rich in autobiographical anecdote. In 1898 an edition of the *Brief Lives* by J. Aubrey,[38] (1626–97), edited by A. Clark, appeared which contains some highly interesting material on Petty. It is widely quoted by Fitzmaurice and reprinted completely in Geoffrey Keynes's bibliography.

Shortly after the publication of the Fitzmaurice biography (reviewed by Higgs[39] in the *Economic Journal*) and of the edition of the *Economic Works* edited by Hull, a number of papers on Petty the economist appeared, in particular an article by Hull[40] and a book by M. Pasquier in French.[41]

After the publication in 1927–8 of the *Petty Papers* and of the *Petty-Southwell Correspondence* there was a renewal of the debate over the attribution of the *Natural and Political Observations* published in 1662 under John Graunt's name. This debate is almost as old as the work itself, for it was initiated by some of Petty's friends who recognized it as his work. The long and detailed story, and detailed bibliography of the debate, can be found in an article by S. Matsukawa.[42] An intermediate position between the obviously partial assessment favoring Petty given by Fitzmaurice and Lansdowne, and the marked opposition of M. Greenwood, is that of Hull, who dedicated part of his introduction to the *Economic Writings* to this question. His authoritative and equilibrated judgment still commands respect. Hull maintains that although Petty offered considerable aid and assistance to his friend in drafting the work, it should nonetheless be considered as substantially the work of Graunt. A wider assessment of Petty, albeit within the context of this debate, is the German work of W. Muller published in 1932.[43] E.A.J. Johnson dedicated a chapter of his now famous book *Predecessors of Adam Smith*, which was published at about the same time, to Petty's economic thought.[44]

Interest in Petty's work has continued to be episodic in the postwar period. A new biography by Emil Strauss[45] in 1954 did not produce any new revelations on Petty's private life or new interpretations of his work, although it is a well-written book with an interesting interpretation of Petty as a man. The book was reviewed by William Letwin.[46] Finally, several compendia on the history of economic thought mention Petty (Schumpeter, Roll and others). Of particular importance in this regard are the treatments of W. Letwin[47] and M. Bowley.[48] Notice should also be drawn to the two-volume work of S. Matsukawa, *Sir William Petty, A Study of the Formation of his Arithmetic-Political Anatomy* published in Japanese (Tokyo, 1958, 1964) but summarized in English by Matsukawa in 1965.[49] The same author has recently discovered an important manuscript among Petty's unpublished papers. It has been published (Matsukawa, 1977) under the title *A Dialogue on Political Arithmetic*, and was probably written around 1670. In Italian, besides the brief mention by Luigi Einaudi,[50] of particular interest is the analysis of G. Pietranera[51] and the review of the collection of Petty's writings translated into Italian by U. Cerroni.[52] More recently, a short paper on Petty was presented by P. Bora at the Fifth International Congress on the Enlightenment.[53]

Finally, the revival of interest in the quantity theory of money brought about by the spread of monetarism and the associated interest in empirical estimation of the velocity of circulation in these monetary-based theories has revived interest in Petty's role as an originator of the concept and an innovator in its estimation (see, e.g., Holtrop[54] and Selden[55]).

2

Political Arithmetic and the Method of Economic Science

2.1 According to a number of historians of economic thought the contribution that set Petty apart from his contemporaries was his role as the founder of political arithmetic.[1] Now, it is generally accepted among economists that the birth of economics as a science occurred in 1776 with the publication of Adam Smith's *Wealth of Nations*. Acceptance of this position implicitly leads to the consideration of political arithmetic as something different from political economy; indeed it is sometimes suggested that it represents a form of analysis closer to statistics (or more precisely economic statistics or demography), if not an early and primitive phase in the development of that branch of science.[2] To anyone who reads Petty's work, however, such a conception would appear to misrepresent his contribution to political economy, and even to favor mistaken ideas about the very meaning of economics as a science. Further investigation of this problem should help us to understand why a historian of economic thought of Marx's stature should have preferred to attribute the title of the "father of English political economy" to Petty rather than to Adam Smith,[3] and at the same time further understanding of the nature of the science and the method of research most appropriate to it.

The source of the misunderstandings concerning the real significance of Petty's work may in part be traced to the term that he coined to represent his method: "political arithmetick." From 1672 onwards Petty used the term frequently in correspondence and in his writings: in 1690 his son gave that title to an essay written by Petty in 1671.[4] His basic idea was that the introduction of quantitative methods would produce a more rigorous analysis of social phenomena, as he himself explicitly indicates:

> [Algebra] came out of Arabia by the Moores into Spaine and from thence hither, and W[illiam] P[etty] hath applyed it to other then purely mathematicall matters, viz: to policy by the name of *Political*

Arithmetick by reducing many termes of matter to termes of number, weight, and measure, in order to be handled Mathematically.[5]

In following this path, Petty was doing nothing more than applying to the social sciences the new ideas, and more generally, the new conception of the world then revolutionizing the natural sciences. During the seventeenth century a new quantitative approach to physics was replacing the old physics based on the description of the quality of the sensations associated with physical objects; in all aspects of scientific research the measurement of quantities became the object of inquiry. This reflects the material-mechanical conception of man and of the world proposed, in particular, by Hobbes; the method of inquiry—the logic of the quantities (*logica sive computatio* as Hobbes said)—corresponds to the very nature of the object being investigated.

The development of the new methodological criteria was accompanied by a radical critique of traditional culture which had been dominated by Aristotelian thought. In this respect the work of Bacon, one of the few authors that Petty cites, and for whom he expresses great admiration, is of even more relevance than that of Hobbes.[6] In opposition to the syllogistic-deductive method of the Aristotelian tradition and the Renaissance tradition of pure empiricism (technicians and alchemists), Bacon proposes the inductive method, a fusion of empiricism and rationalism:

> the empiricists, like ants, are content to amass and then consume; the rationalists, like spiders, construct a web from their cerebral matter. It is bees who follow a middle way: first extracting the raw material from the flowers of the gardens and fields, they then transform it, elaborating it by virtue of their own activity. Similarly, the action of true philosophy should use not only, or above all, mental forces, and should not limit itself to committing to memory intact the material furnished by natural history and by the mechanical experiments, but should collect it in the intellect, transformed and elaborated.[7]

This is precisely the method followed by Petty who does not limit himself to the description of social phenomena in quantitative terms but also, and above all, attempts to give rational explanation to the assembled data. Indeed, he often goes so far as to attempt to reconstruct the data required for an investigation on the basis of complicated chains of deductive reasoning of an arithmetic-quantitative nature that permit the scarce available information to be exploited for a myriad of different purposes and which themselves constitute an excellent applied example of the new logic of quantities.

Further, Petty emphasizes his decision to base his own analysis on *objective* data. This position is also representative of a widely accepted tendency within the new scientific approach, but Petty's explicit affirmations on the subject take on particular importance because his investigations were undertaken in the area of the humane, rather than the natural, sciences. In this respect a famous passage from the Preface of his *Political Arithmetick*, published posthumously in 1690, can be considered as his "declaration of intent":

> The Method I take to do this, is not yet very usual; for instead of using only comparative and superlative words, and intellectual Arguments, I have taken the course (as a Specimen of the Political Arithmetick I have long aimed at) to express my self in Terms of *Number*, *Weight*, or *Measure*; to use only Arguments of Sense, and to consider only such Causes, as have visible Foundations in Nature; leaving those that depend upon the mutable Minds, Opinions, Appetites and Passions of particular Men, to the Consideration of others. . . .[8]

As can be seen from the testimony of his own words, Petty's analysis represents a net contrast with the logico-deductive method of the Scholastics which was still dominant, if not all pervasive, in questions of scientific research in the seventeenth century. It is necessary, however, to qualify this point by recalling that for Petty it was not only a question of *recording* and *describing* reality "in terms of number, weight or measure," but rather to *express* reality in such terms in order to identify its principal characteristics and thus to be in a position to place at the basis of his own theory "only such causes, as have visible foundations in nature," that is *objective*, rather than *subjective*, causes.

The tendency to direct research towards the identification of precise quantitative interrelationships between the phenomena under study can be only vaguely perceived in the work of Bacon, but is already developed by the time of Hobbes and a few contemporary men of science. The first to clearly express his intentions in this respect was Galileo according to whom "this great book which is open in front of our eyes—I mean the Universe— . . . is written in mathematical characters"[9]; knowledge of the world therefore required the construction of arithmetic or geometric models (Hobbes insists in particular on the latter in his work). Petty also adopts such a point of view, although with more qualification, and as we shall see (in chapter 8, section 2) even proposed some econometric relationships, such as that relating the price of a commodity to a number of its physical characteristics. Further, a conception of the world similar to that of Galileo and Hobbes is reflected in the formula "number, weight or measure" which is continuously present in Petty's work, and to which we shall return in the next section. Political arithmetic was not only considered as the most appropriate instrument for the description of reality, but also for interpreting reality precisely because, according to the materialistic-mechanical conception supported by Galileo and Hobbes, reality expresses itself by means of a quantitative structure.

Another essential element of the new methodological approach that Petty adopted[10] was the sharp separation between science and morals which was necessary for the domination of man over nature asserted by Bacon in his *Instauratio magna* and enthusiastically adopted by Hobbes: the moral problem could not arise for science which was simply a means; although it did pertain to the ends that man proposed to attain by means of the utilization of the results of science. This is a position that has maintained dominance up to our own day, although not without periods of marked dissension (consider the debate on atomic energy) and that has been of decisive importance to the development of the humane sciences.[11]

Within the context of the general framework presented in this section we can proceed, in the remaining sections, to give Petty's methodological position more precision. The first problem that requires more detailed discussion (in section 2.2) is the problem that has just been alluded to: the relation between scientific research and practical action, between the laws of nature and positive laws. It will then be possible to try (in section 2.3) to give more exact meaning to Petty's formula "number, weight, or measure" in order to show how it necessarily led him to conceive of the study of economic phenomena in systematic form, as the manifestation of the activity of a unified "body politick." Finally, in setting out an overview (in section 2.4) of the general lines that our discussion will follow in the succeeding chapters, we will give a provisional evaluation of how far the "systemic requirements" implicit in Petty's methodological approach were translated into effective analytical results.

2.2 The first aspect that has to be clarified concerns the practical motivations for Petty's investigations. As we have already had the occasion to point out, his choice of subjects for investigation, as well as the positions he sought to support, were closely connected to his personal interests.

Petty frequently emphasized the disinterested nature of his investigations. It is a point to which he returns on any number of occasions, even in papers that were certainly not intended for publication, such as his correspondence with Southwell. However, this insistence was simply a reflection of the moral customs of the period in which the general public was not always capable of following the logic of the arguments or verifying the data employed, and had been rendered suspicious by the all-too-frequent cases of apparently scientific writings providing partisan support for specific private interests.[12] For this reason writers dealing with the affairs of government had gotten into the habit of initiating their works with protestations of innocence and assurances of their disinterest in the subjects they treated. It is certainly possible that Petty wrote his essays "for my curiosity," as he says, for example, in the Preface to *The Political Arithmetic of Ireland*[13]; but such protestations are in direct contrast with the eminently practical character of his published work. The relation to current political events is even pointed out in a number of places by Petty himself[14] and it is certainly not by chance that his essays regularly concluded with a series of proposals directed to the King or some other high-placed public authority.

Petty's behavior raises the age-old question of the possibility of man improving the course of human events. Petty presented this question as a problem of the relation between positive laws, attempts by governments to regulate the operation of the social system, and natural laws. He thus commits the error common to all the pre-Marxian classical economists of identifying the "laws" of the behavior of a particular historically determined mode of production—capitalism—with natural laws.[15] For example, his comparisons, influenced by his medical training, between the human body and the body politic, have this intention.[16] But, Petty does not transform his confusion between "economic laws" and the laws of nature into a position of absolute liberalism. This error is overcome by the "natural common sense" of a social reformer who, without necessarily considering the existing social order as eternal, is not led to question its existence because he is striving to bring about its definitive consolidation. He is thus led to consider it as a given to be placed at the basis of his analysis. (Such a position, which today might be defined as conservative, must be considered, given the historical period in which Petty was active, as progressive even if it was not one of rupture.) Petty was thus a firm believer in the possibility of influencing economic reality, and that the effects could be positive if only the spontaneous tendencies at work in the system were taken into account in framing policy. In the absence of adequate knowledge of the actual operation of the system, and of what the probable long-run as well as immediate effects of potential economic policy measures would be, Petty believed that it was more opportune to abstain from policy intervention.

As one might expect of a writer as rapid and prolific as Petty, the position spelled out above is in fact derived from statements, a number of which are at least apparently contradictory with each other. Petty could support liberal positions, while at the same time a very torrent of proposals for state intervention in the economy flowed from his pen. For example, in the Preface to *A Treatise of Taxes and Contributions* he states:

> I would now advertise [to] the world, that I do not think I can mend it, and that I hold it best for every man's particular quiet, to let it *vadere sicut vult*; I know well, that *res nolunt male administrari*, and that (say I what I will or can) things will have their course, nor will nature be couzened.[17]

But clear-cut statements such as this are qualified in other passages. For example, in *A Treatise of Taxes and Contributions*, where Petty compares the politician who intervenes in the economic system with the physician who operates on the human body, he limits himself to recommending caution, and implicitly admits the opportunity of a degree of intervention by the physician-politician:

> We must consider in general, that as wiser Physicians tamper not excessively with their Patients, rather observing and complying with the motions of nature, then contradicting it with vehement Administrations of their own; so in Politicks and Oconomicks, the same must be used; for *Naturam expellas furca licet usque recurrit*.[18]

Certain interventions are thus justified by the necessity of making positive laws consistent with natural laws, as in the Preface of *A Treatise of Taxes and Contributions* where Petty points out that the work is being presented to the public in a moment in which, for various reasons, "there is opportunity, to pass into Positive Laws whatsoever is right reason and the Law of Nature."[19] This position implies a particular conception of the "Law of Nature": not laws that are irresistibly established by the inexorable operation of autonomous forces and about which it is useless to make value judgments ("laws of nature" in the sense of physics or chemistry), but rather objectives or goals toward which one strives because of their desirability although it would always be possible to impede such movement or even to move in the opposite direction. In practice Petty considered as a law of nature everything that facilitated the proper functioning of the developing capitalist system, e.g., the repeated proposals for a land registry, which was meant to guarantee certainty over private property of the means of production; the abolition of customs barriers within the kingdom (and in particular those between England and Ireland) in order to encourage economic development; the creation of financial intermediaries (banks) to ease the process of accumulation; and wage legislation to keep wages as low as possible. We have already mentioned these proposals, and will discuss them more fully below[20]; here it is sufficient to point out that the "law of nature" has a rather different significance in Petty's work than it would come to have somewhat later in the work of Ricardo and his followers, and above all in that of more recent or present-day marginalist economics. Given the historical epoch in which he lived and worked, adherence to the law of nature for Petty signified approval of the great social and economic developments that were then taking place. Paraphrasing Marx we could say that Petty's proposals aimed at "the removal of all legally removable hindrances to the free development of the *bourgeoisie*."[21]

2.3 It can thus be seen that Petty's investigations were not meant to produce a general knowledge of the world—pure and simple, comprehensive description of reality—but rather were more or less directly stimulated by the practical problems of the day and were intended to serve as guides for policy. This is the first element leading to a more precise understanding of the specific meaning that Petty attached to the formula "number, weight or measure" which is in itself open to various interpretations. Of biblical origin,[22] it has been used in a completely different context by Pufendorf,[23] while Petty's declared followers such as King and Davenant seem to have interpreted it simplistically, as nothing more than the recording and description of quantitative phenomena. That this was not Petty's interpretation is demonstrated by, among other things, his explicit recognition that as a description of reality, political arithmetic was necessarily imperfect.[24] Petty's admission precedes that of Adam Smith (see above, note 2) and coming, as it does, from the founder of the science, takes on a rather different aspect. It should not be considered as a rejection in principle of a method of research, but rather as a specification of its limits and its real objectives. Political arithmetic serves its purpose to the extent that it allows the collection of the essential elements of the designated object of analysis:

> 'Tis true, that curious Dissections cannot be made without variety
> of proper Instruments; whereas I have had only a commin Knife and a
> Clout, instead of the many more helps which such a Work requires:
> However, my rude approaches being enough to find whereabout the
> Liver and Spleen, and Lungs lye, tho' not to discern the Lymphatick
> Vessels. . . .[25]

Petty then is not interested in furnishing a description of reality that
even though approximate will nonetheless tend eventually to the ultimate objective of an absolute correspondence with the object being
described (a "map" of reality with a scale of one to one, which would
be not only impossible to draw up, but also useless as a theoretical or
practical guide). Without losing himself in a sea of detailed information, Petty sets out to identify the fundamental aspects of the problem
being studied, abstracting from useless elements and facts of minor
importance which, as Ricardo would have occasion to express the
matter a century and a half later, produce only "modification" in the
analysis, but do not change the substance of the conclusions.[26]

In order to avoid misunderstanding, it would perhaps be better not to
use the term "political arithmetic" to represent the essence of Petty's
approach to research since it lends itself too readily, as we have already
seen, to interpretation as the simple process of collecting statistics.
There is an alternative to the term, employed by Petty himself in the
title of another of his books, which would seem to be much more
appropriate: "political anatomy." In the Preface to *The Political
Anatomy of Ireland* Petty explains just exactly what he means by the
term:

> Sir Francis Bacon, in his *Advancement of Learning*, hath made a
> judicious Parallel in many particulars, between the Body Natural,
> and Body Politick, and between the Arts of preserving both in Health
> and Strength: And it is as reasonable, that as Anatomy is the best
> foundation of one, so also of the other; and that to practice upon the
> Politick, without knowing the Symmetry, Fabrick, and Proportion of
> it, is as casual as the practice of Old-Women and Empyricks.[27]

The triad "symmetry, fabric and proportion" of political anatomy
corresponds to the "number, weight or measure" of political
arithmetic: Petty is attempting to furnish a selective interpretation of
the complexity of the real world, and to highlight the essential factors in
the functioning of the "body politick." The distinctive characteristic
of Petty's work, relative to the majority of contemporary authors, is

represented precisely by his recognition of the fact that the various economic problems confronted—whether it is a question of money, or of international trade, or any other subject—should not be considered independently, but as an integral part of a larger whole.

2.4 It is this "systemic nature" that puts Petty a step above his contemporaries and constitutes his principal claim to the title of "the founder of modern political economy." It will be our task in the chapters which follow to attempt to verify the extent to which Petty's analysis can be considered a faithful and adequate realization of the idea of the "body politick" which constitutes its unifying theme.

Naturally, this evaluation can be attempted only after an assessment and analysis of Petty's currently available works. However, some preliminary indications may be useful at this point to indicate the line of development of the subsequent chapters.

Keeping in mind the historical period in which Petty lived, marked by the development of commercial capitalism, the beginning of the agricultural revolution, but only early signs of the incipient industrial revolution, it is possible to identify the limitations of his analysis. At one extreme we find a substantially correct conception of the role of money; at the other a theory of prices which is undermined by failure to consider adequately the interdependencies linking the various productive sectors one to the other and the tendency of capitalistic competition to produce uniformity in the rate of profits earned in the various sectors. In the succeeding chapters we will follow this order precisely, beginning with those areas in which Petty's analytical conception best reflects his "systemic" conception of the "political system": money (chapter 3), international trade (chapter 4) and the fiscal system (chapter 5). The failure to recognize the importance of the problem of relative prices, today considered as the "theoretical nucleus" or the "core" of political economy, and the consequent failure to provide a solution to the problem obviously limits the analytical apparatus applied in the areas of research treated in chapters 3, 4, and 5. However, the nature of Petty's investigations, meant to furnish a general framework for the understanding of the functioning of the "body politick" can, at least as a first approximation, be considered independently of such problems that require a correct treatment of the problem of relative prices. This allows us, after having already assembled and examined various elements which will be helpful in understanding Petty's system of thought, to take into consideration, among other things, the problem of the operative mechanisms that lie behind the laws of development of the economic system, (chapters 6 and 7), and the problem of value and of relative prices (chapter 8). We will thus be able to offer a more reasoned evaluation, in the concluding chapter, of the problem raised at the beginning of this section, namely, the merits and limitations of the "systemic nature" of Petty's analysis, and thus of the extent of his contribution to the birth of political economy.

3

Money

3.1 The importance that pre-Smithian economists attributed to money is well known. It was generally considered as the essential component of wealth, whose acquisition was the primary aim of international trade. This conception, which the historians of economic thought usually contrast to the classical idea of money as a veil, was undoubtedly influenced by the conditions then prevailing. Of particular importance was the interdependence (which was only beginning to be alleviated by the nascent system of financial intermediation) between a number of prerequisites of the industrial revolution, such as the development of commerce and the accumulation of private wealth, and the availability of gold and silver. The theoretical expression of this state of affairs occasionally went much further, attributing excessive importance to the quantity of gold and silver possessed by the sovereign and his subjects.[1]

Petty's analysis is of extreme interest from this point of view. He intuitively sensed, and his work expressed, the historical necessity of his age while at the same time demonstrating a great deal of good sense, avoiding in large part the errors committed by his contemporaries. Petty expresses the substance of his conception of money by drawing a parallel, which was usual at the time, between political anatomy and human anatomy which differs only slightly, but very significantly, from the traditional parallel between money and blood:[2]

> Money is but the Fat of the Body-politick, whereof too much doth as often hinder its Agility, as too little makes it sick. 'Tis true, that as Fat lubricates the motion of the Muscles, feeds in want of Victuals, fills up uneven Cavities, and beautifies the Body, so doth Money in the State quicken its Action, feeds from abroad in the time of Dearth at Home; evens accounts by reason of its divisibility, and beautifies the whole, altho more especially the particular persons that have it in plenty.[3]

Of the three functions generally attributed to money (unit of measure, medium of exchange, store of value) it is the second that is here given pride of place. The first is also discussed by Petty in a number of places in his writings,[4] while the third may be seen implicitly in the criterion of durability that Petty employs to explain why gold and silver are the most suitable representations of wealth.[5] In the pages that follow we will examine in greater detail Petty's point of view on the three functions of money (sections 3.2, 3.3, 3.4), some implications for economic policy related to foreign trade, and finally, the level of the rate of interest will be discussed (section 3.5).

3.2 Petty recognizes the conventional nature of the function of money as a unit of measure, and at the same time denies that money constitutes an *absolute* measure:

> Money is understood to be the uniform Measure and Rule for Value of all Commodities. But whether in that sense there be any Money, or such Rule in the World, I know not . . . tho most are persuaded that Gold and Silver Money is such. For 1. The proportion of value between pure Gold and fine Silver, alters as the Earth and Industry of Men produce more of one than of the other. . . .
> 2. The value of Silver rises and falls it self . . . Now the Accidents of so doing, make Silver rise and fall, and consequently take from the perfect Aptitude for being an uniform steady Rule and Measure of all other things.[6]

In this brief passage, the contents of which are reaffirmed at various other points in his writings,[7] Petty sets out his position on two of the most hotly debated issues of his age: the nature of money (a commodity or a paper symbol), and bimetallism.[8] On the first question Petty's position appears to be similar to those who considered money as a commodity, such as Smith and Ricardo somewhat later. He was, however, aware of the fiduciary operations of banks:

> Money is an artificiall Thing or rather No Thing though Solomon sayes it answers all Things, but Is rather the Signe of a Thing. For if men were excellently Versed in accompts Money were not necessary at all and many places as Barbados &c. have made shift without it & so they do in Banks.[9]

Thus, although he affirms that "Nor were it hard to substitute in the place of Money (were a competency of it wanting) what should be equivalent unto it,"[10] his practical proposals in this regard, such as the land bank which will be discussed more fully below, all tend to guarantee a real base (land, jewels, etc.) to the fiduciary circulation. For Petty the value of money depended on the value of the precious metal (or of commodities in general) that they contain or represent; only a "few . . . Fools . . . take Money by its name, and not by its weight and fineness."[11] Thus, if the gold or silver content of money were reduced, prices should increase in the same proportion.[12]

Petty's position on the question of bimetallism is derived logically from his views on the nature of money. Variations in the relative values of gold and silver caused by changes in costs and quantities produced would produce changes in the relative values of gold money relative to silver money. As a consequence there should be only a single unit or measure.[13] The attempt to maintain a bimetallic system would only lead o speculation which would drive out of circulation the money whose real value (value of the embodied metal) was higher than its nominal value.[14]

3.3 Petty clearly recognizes the importance of the second function of money as an instrument to ease the circulation of commodities. He continually emphasizes the damage that a scarcity of money can have on the level of productive activity.[15] It is within this context that Petty confronts the problem of the determination of the quantity of money necessary to support the commercial activity of a nation. One should therefore guard against the temptation to interpret Petty's work from the viewpoint of the Quantity theory of money since the principal proposition of that theory concerns the relation between the quantity of money and the level of prices. Petty does not even recognize such a relation. Instead, he considers the principal influence of the available quantity of money to be on the level of activity, as has just been pointed out, and on the rate of interest, as will be discussed in section 3.5. The problem of the optimal· quantity of money is thus approached as a problem of the determination of the most suitable physical composition of national wealth from the viewpoint of the overall productivity of the system.[16] Money is considered as an indirect cost of production, a cost which corresponds to the value of precious metals embodied in the stock of money. For this reason an excess of money constitutes waste, even if it creates less serious problems than a shortage of money, because the surplus of precious metals could have been exchanged for means of production, if not directly employed in production process.[17] In this respect Petty's proposals to reduce the quantity of precious metals necessary for the monetary circulation, such as the creation of the land bank,[18] can be interpreted as propositions for institutional engineering which, if applied, would have constituted a form of technical progress inasmuch as they would have led to a reduction in the (indirect) costs necessary for a given economic system to produce a given flow of income.

Petty's principal contribution in this area is his use of the velocity of circulation concept to determine the optimal quantity of money: " . . . the Expence being 40 Millions, if the revolutions were in such short Circles, *viz.* weekly, as happens among poorer artisans and labourers, who receive and pay every *Saturday*, then 40/52 parts of 1 Million of Money would answer those ends: But if the Circles be quarterly, according to our Custom of paying rent, and gathering Taxes, then 10 Millions were requisite. Wherefore supposing payments in general to be of a mixed Circle between One week and 13 then add 10 Millions to 40/52, the half of which will be 5 1/2 , so as if we have 5 1/2 Millions we have enough."[19]

As may be seen in the passage just given, Petty estimated the velocity of circulation on the basis of the institutional characteristics of the economic system such as the payments periods for wages, rents, and taxes. It is not surprising that an economist writing before the development of financial intermediation should consider the determination of the velocity of circulation primarily from an institutional standpoint, nor that he should be completely blind to the factor given so much emphasis by Keynes: the importance of the speculative demand for money (connected to money's function as a store of value) in determining the velocity of circulation. There can be little doubt that the considerable degree of flexibility in the current financial system admits the possibility that changes in the demand for liquidity in the system to some extent be met with changes in the velocity of circulation. However, there can be little doubt that Petty's position is closer to the reality of the seventeenth century. On the other hand, Petty's clear perception of the velocity of circulation of money concept is present in only very few subsequent writers of that epoch, such as Locke and Cantillon.[20]

3.4 From what has been said in the previous section it is evident that while an overabundance of money can be easily eliminated by means of melting down the excess coin, scarcity of money requires institutional reform (creation of banks) or a long period of balance of payments surpluses in order to be eliminated. It is thus easy to understand why Petty, in agreement with the views of his contemporaries, was much more willing to sanction an excess than a deficiency of money.[21] However, his belief that a nation can have too much, just as easily as too little, money and that scarcity could be eliminated by policies other than a surplus on the balance of payments, produced a much more flexible position with respect to international trade. For example, Petty realistically considered the prohibition of the export of money to be useless:

> The danger of it resolves either into a kinde of Ensurance answerable to the danger of being seized, or unto a surcharge of a Composition by bribing the Searchers.[22]

At the same time, although Petty was very favorably disposed to the import of money resulting from a positive trade balance[23] or from the import of foreign capital,[24] he did not consider these as absolute priorities, considering them as subordinate to the objective of a high level of employment. In this respect he was willing to go so far as to accept the export of money and reject import restrictions even in conditions of a small deficit in the balance of trade.[25] We shall return to these topics in the next chapter which is dedicated to the problem of international trade. Here it is sufficient to emphasize that for Petty the accumulation of precious metals was not an end in itself, but the means to an end. This position is clarified in the same passages in which Petty expresses his position in favor of a surplus on the balance of payments: "Gold and Silver . . . are not only not perishable, but are esteemed for Wealth at all times, and every where: Whereas other Commodities which are perishable, or whose value depends upon the Fashion; or which are contingently scarce and plentiful, are wealth, but *pro hic et nunc*. . . .[26]

As Marx, who quotes this passage, correctly remarks, Petty does not identify money with wealth, nor does he go to the opposite extreme of considering precious metals as commodities just like all others. Rather, gold and silver are correctly considered "as the material representative and general form of wealth."[27] From this point of view the accumulation of gold and silver can be considered as the original and general form of accumulation.[28] Even if the limitations of Petty's conception of accumulation reflects the primitive form of capitalist development that he experienced, it should not be forgotten that some passages of his writings foresee the more advanced form of capitalist development, the accumulation of capital, and the superiority of this form with respect to the simple accumulation of money:

> Question: Is not a Country the Poorer for having less Money?
> Answer: Not always: For as the most thriving Men keep little or no Money by them, but turn and wind it into various Commodities to their great Profit, so may the whole Nation also; which is but many particular Men united.[29]

The accumulation of precious metals thus has a sense precisely because, in the form of money, it has a third function in addition to being the measure of value and medium of exchange: that of being the "general form of wealth" as Marx put it, or as the "store of value" according to the more specific, but less rich, Keynesian terminology.

3.5 The last aspect of Petty's theory of money that remains to be discussed is his theory of interest. Petty defines interest (or the use of money) as "A Reward for forbearing the use of your own Money for a Term of Time agreed upon, whatsoever need your self may have of it in the mean while."[30] This position should first be recognized as a statement on the centuries-old argument concerning the legitimacy of interest,[31] "forbearing" providing a moral justification for the charges of bankers and usurers. The "amount" of "forbearance" could also have provided the basis of a subjective theory of the level of the rate of interest, but Petty's methodological position made this impossible. Instead he explained the level of this premium of forbearing, which constitutes the "pure" rate of interest, by reference to an "objective" element, the return to an equivalent investment in real estate:

> As for Usury, the least that can be, is the Rent of so much Land as the money lent will buy, where the security is undoubted . . . .[32]

Then there is a second component to interest which must be added to the first which Petty indicates in the continuation of the passage just cited:

> but where the security is casual, then a kind of ensurance must be enterwoven with the simple natural interest.[33]

It is on the basis of this risk premium "which may advance the Usury very conscionably unto any height below the Principal it self" that Petty based his arguments against all attempts to limit the level of the rate of interest by means of legislation.[34] This position is analogous to that which he regularly adopted towards every such attempt at legislative regulation of economic phenomena: "natural laws" cannot be violated by human laws.[35] This should not be taken to imply that Petty was indifferent to the level of the rate of interest. An excessively high rate of interest was considered to be a brake on economic activity and a cause of high prices which damage exports.[36] A low rate of interest is thus one of the factors that combine to assure the prosperity of a country, although it is in general more correct to say that low interest is the effect, and not the cause, of such prosperity, in particular the abundance of money.[37] Petty did, however, consider that the level of the rate of interest could be influenced by policy. For example, it might be reduced by means of institutional changes which could reduce risk (such as the land register, which would make it possible to control accurately the collateral offered by the borrower to the lender) or by bringing about an increase in the quantity of money available for lending (through a land bank).[38]

Petty thus expresses with incisive intelligence and good sense the complexity of a phenomenon that is simultaneously cause and effect in a given situation. He is able to take into account the existence of a network of interdependencies in which every variable depends on the combined action of all the others without letting this complexity prevent the identification of the more important causal relationships. Petty's insightful recognition of the importance of the institutional context for the functioning of the economy allowed him to build on these relationships to produce significant policy recommendations.

4

International Trade

4.1 Petty's ideas on international trade have already been referred to in relation to the discussion of money in the previous chapter. There it was pointed out that although Petty shared the position then dominant among his contemporaries concerning the desirability of a surplus on the balance of payments as an instrument to attract precious metals to the country, he qualified his position so as to avoid errors such as the identification of the precious metals with national wealth, which liberal historians of economic thought attribute to the so-called "mercantilists."[1] For Petty, a surplus on the balance of payments, with the inflow of precious metals which follows as a consequence, was a desirable, but subordinate, objective to a high level of employment and internal production. The superiority of gold, silver, and jewels over other goods was only relative and explained by their durability and their role as money which gave them the attribute of general representations of wealth, a necessary prerequisite for the accumulation of capital.[2] In addition, wages were highest in those sectors involved in international trade, a factor which may be explained, as we shall see more clearly below, by the importance of the international trade in the initial phases of capitalistic development.[3] Petty also recognizes other advantages of international trade, such as the possibility of mitigating the effects of crises caused by accidental events and striking individual countries.[4] More important was the incentive to the development of the division of labor caused by the expansion of the market. This would tend to increase productivity, making domestic products more competitive in world markets, and producing further expansion in international trade.[5] Finally, a strong trading country would find it easier to convert men and equipment rapidly to the needs of war, in particular sailors and ships.[6]

In spite of all of this, however, Petty was not led to call for policies, such as those found in nearly all the economic literature of the sixteenth and the beginning of the seventeenth centuries, which should guarantee a positive trade balance in every sector and with all countries. On the contrary, he considered that policies prohibiting the export of money and precious metals could be damaging in certain conditions and in any case useless because they were unenforceable.[7] Among Petty's various proposals was a recommendation to reduce imports through substitution of domestically produced goods, which satisfies both the objective of a positive trade balance and increased domestic employment.[8] The passages in which Petty refuses to condemn the importation of even luxuries and nondurable consumption goods, if this permits the export of domestically produced goods which would otherwise not find a market, indicate that employment was considered the principal objective. As has already been seen in the previous chapter, Petty's primary objective was not a surplus on the balance of payments, which was in fact only considered as the means to his principal objective: a high and increasing level of productive activity. To this end Petty considers favorably the importation of foreign capital and the immigration of skilled foreign laborers, condemning any legislation prohibiting or impeding such movements.[9]

This brief review of the role that Petty assigned to international trade allows the closer examination of some more specific questions related to the subject, such as the elements of the theory of international trade based on absolute costs which is implicit in Petty's work, and discussion of the problem of customs duties (in section 4.2), as well as the problem of the existence of internal customs duties and the question of the colonies (in section 4.3). Finally, in concluding this short chapter we shall consider briefly the problem of the determination of rates of exchange (section 4.4).

4.2 Petty's theory of international exchange is based on absolute costs. World markets are controlled by those countries that benefit from natural or acquired advantages which allow them to produce at lower costs and thus to sell their goods in international markets at lower prices than other countries.[10] Since interest is considered among the relevant costs, a rate of interest lower than that prevailing in competing countries presents an important advantage in international trade because it permits traders to earn profits, net of interest payments, even when they charge prices that are below those of competitors in other countries.[11] Among the measures most advantageous to English exports, Petty gives prominence to those that aim at the reduction of the production costs of primary necessities.[12]

The prices paid by the buyers of exported and imported goods will also be affected by customs duties which can be set so as to encourage a trade surplus:

> The Measures of Customs outwards may be such, as after reason-
> able profit to the Exporter will leave such of our own Commodities
> as are necessary to Forreigners somewhat cheaper unto them then
> they can be had from elsewhere.

On the other hand,

> The Measures of Customs upon imported Commodities are: 1.
> That all things ready and ripe for Consumption may be made some-
> what dearer then the same things grown or made at home, if the same
> be feasible *ceteris paribus*. 2. That all Superfluities tending to Luxury
> and sin, might be loaded with so much Impost, as to serve instead of a
> sumptuary Law to restrain the use of them. But here also care is to be
> had that it be not better to smuckle then to pay.[13]

Any difference between the price in the world market and the domestic production price (equal to cost plus an ''adequate'' profit) should
then be almost completely absorbed by export duties. This proposal
reflects Petty's position that the greater productivity and the relative
advantage are due to the ''merit'' of the State as a whole.

Imports, especially of finished products, should be obstructed by
duties on such goods which would form an integral part of a system of
proportional tax on expenditure recommended, as shall be seen in the
next chapter, by Petty as the most desirable system of taxation.[14] In
general, and in the absence of grave problems on the balance of payments, Petty viewed a system of high customs duties with disfavor. In
this respect he refers to Holland, where the duties are so low, both for
imports and exports, as to serve above all else as a means of providing
adequate statistics on foreign trade flows.[15] Indeed, in the case of low
duties, statistics will be even more reliable because smuggling will be
less profitable. The government then disposes of a more reliable measure for judging the state of international payments and is better able to
judge the opportunity of restrictive action to control imports (in particular to prohibit the import of luxury goods) or to favoring the
substitution of internal production for imports.[16]

Petty identifies an alternative method for discouraging the importation of luxury goods based on the observation that such goods are
destined to a restricted part of the population. Using simple common
sense he anticipates the modern *demonstration effect*, adapting it in a
typically puritan way to formulate a positive proposal for intervention:

> That the Lord Lieutenant and Council, as also the Nobility, Courts
> of Justice, and Officers of the Army and other Gentlemen in and

about Dublin, may by their engagement and example, discountenance the use of some certain Foreign Commodities, to be pitched upon by your Lordships: And that Gentlemen and Freeholders in the country, at their Assizes, and other Country meetings: and that the Inhabitants of all Corporations, who live in Houses of above two Chimneys in each, may afterwards do the same.[17]

On the other hand, imported raw materials and semifinished goods destined for use as inputs for home production should be spared from excessively high customs duties: "all things not fully wrought and Manufactured, as also all Tools and Materials for Manufacture, as also Dying-stuff, etc., ought to be gently dealt with."[18] In this way, it would be possible to reduce the impact of high prices of necessary means of production on internal production costs, and thus defend the competitivity of domestic products in world markets. Petty thus can be seen to adopt, if only partially, the ideas introduced in France by Colbert to support domestic manufacturers: high duties, if not embargoes, on imports of finished products and exports of raw materials; extremely low duties on imports of raw materials and exports of finished goods.[19] Petty condemned attempts to hinder the export of raw materials, attributing more importance to efforts to increase domestic productivity than to traditional protectionist measures; any attempt to contravene the natural differences in national productivity with measures of an administrative nature, such as duties and embargoes was, in his opinion not only useless but dangerous.[20]

4.3 Finally, there was no question that duties and restrictions on trade within the kingdom were clearly to be condemned; among these the most obvious case was represented by the duties and prohibitions to the importation of Irish grain and meat into England. Such measures produced increased costs for English producers equal to the higher prices that had to be paid for raw materials and the higher wages due to the higher prices to be paid for the means of subsistence; they thus favored imports at the expense of domestic production and, above all, threatened the internal unity of the kingdom.[21]

On the basis of this position, and considering Ireland as the principal colony of England, Petty's views on colonialism can be briefly outlined. From what has just been said, Petty would appear to have been a strong supporter of what would come to be called a "customs union": the various territories should constitute a single market without internal barriers and be regulated by uniform legislation. But, the geographical obstacles to unification of the markets (the distance of the colony from the motherland) and the dispersion of the population (which increases costs of production, and above all the indirect costs of justice and administration) are such that colonies clearly represent a charge on the kingdom.[22] The obstacles to trade between Ireland and England made the payment of rents to the landlords of Irish property, in large part resident in England, even more costly.[23] In this regard, Petty highlights the fact that the balance of payments for a colonized territory will be in substantial deficit even in the presence of a surplus in trade in goods and services:

> A great part of the Estates, both real and personal in Ireland, are owned by Absentees, and such as draw over the profits raised out of Ireland refunding nothing; so as Ireland exporting more then it imports doth yet grow poorer to a paradox.[24]

4.4 It remains to consider the problem of rates of exchange. In a system based on precious metals the rate of exchange between different moneys will vary around the value determined by the relative amounts of gold and silver contained in them. In normal conditions divergences from this value will not exceed the costs of transport of precious metals from one country to another (the so-called "gold points," already discussed in the financial literature of the sixteenth century). Petty, who only concerned himself *en passant* with the problem, did not discuss the automatic mechanism determining the distribution of the precious metals among the various countries, which in any event would not be fully explained until the first half of the eighteenth century.[25] Indeed, he clearly considered that substantial deviations from the natural levels of exchange rates were possible and could be determined by political decision.

In the first place, the costs of the financial operation of transferring money from one country to another[26] could be superior, in extraordinary situations, to the normal level, determined by the cost of transport of money plus insurance against risk. This was the case, for example, of the Irish transfers to England, made excessively costly by the legal obstacles to trade between the two countries.[27]

In the second place, although Petty seemed to accept that measures could be instituted to impose changes in the prices of domestic goods in terms of foreign money, he expressed little confidence in maneuvers of this kind since he considered external demand rigid over the long period:

> Abating our prices will as well allure strangers to buy extraordinary proportions of our Commodities, as raising their money will do: But neither that, nor abating the price will make strangers use more

of our Commodities then they want; for although the first year they should carry away an unuseful and superfluous proportion, yet afterwards they would take so much the less.[28]

As can be seen from these brief indications, Petty's analysis of international exchange is primitive and fragmentary. Contrary to what the traditional classification of Petty as a mercantilist economist (a term that, as Schumpeter points out, is entirely inadequate to cover a substantially heterogeneous group of authors) might lead one to believe, international trade is not the center of his attention. It is not in this area that one should expect to find Petty's contribution to the birth of economic science.[29]

5

The Fiscal System

5.1 The institution of the modern State is implicitly recognized, as we shall see more clearly in chapter 6, in Petty's analysis as a necessary precondition for that qualitative jump in the process of economic development represented by the birth of capitalism. And Petty, perhaps more than many of his contemporaries who were primarily involved in discussions of the importance of a surplus in international trade and the acceptability of usury, clearly recognized the importance of a reform of the taxation system as the first step in assuring the uniformity of conditions within a country, and certainty over the economic rules of the game, necessary for the development of economic activity based on private initiative.

According to the assessment of one of the most respected students of Petty's work, Petty's ideas on the various aspects of taxation "constitute a coherent whole."[1] In fact, more important than the various points in which Petty's analysis anticipates modern developments, the modern student of public finance will be more interested in his continual attempts to spell out the relationships that exist between the problem of taxation and public expenditure on the one hand and the various other problems considered in the analysis on the other, which allowed fiscal relations to play an organic role in Petty's overall representation of the functioning of the economic system.

In the pages that follow we will rapidly examine this aspect of Petty's approach, leaving to one side his specific analysis of the various categories of government receipts and expenditures to concentrate attention on problems of greater importance for the study of political economy. We will first examine Petty's ideas on the optimal conditions for a system of taxation which, compared with the chaotic regulations that existed at the time, spell out a modern institutional framework suitable to the nascent capitalist mode of production (sections 5.2 and 5.3). Section 5.4 is dedicated to the analysis of some particular types of taxation, such as the depreciation of the currency and customs duties. Finally, we shall look at the relation between taxes and public expenditures, in particular as it effects the creation of wealth and the level of employment (section 5.5).

5.2 The largest part of Petty's *A Treatise of Taxes and Contributions* is concerned with the systematic examination of the various types of government income, and he returns to this aspect of the question in various places in his other work. The picture that he paints is of an intricate labyrinth of often self-contradictory regulations which were clearly detrimental, in their overall effect, to the development of economic activity. Emphasizing this situation, Petty considered the system for procuring government income, then in practice, to be one of the major "impediments of England's Greatness," while at the same time insisting that these obstacles "are but contingent and removable."[2] The "impediments" to the system that he describes to his readers derive, according to Petty, from the stratification caused by continuous additions to the initial system which, as a result, no longer serves its original purpose and loses its initial coherence.[3] Thus, the burden of taxation is born almost exclusively, and with a varying and unpredictable intensity, by the landowner and depends on "the casual predominancy of Parties and Factions." In addition, the cost of collection, subcontracted to private agents, was very high and introduced further elements of injustice and uncertainty into the system.[4] Naturally, it would be impossible to rationalize the system by returning it to its original state, and Petty guards himself against proposals of this nature, even if such a solution would have been consistent with his explanation of the defects of the system in terms of the accumulation of "impediments" within a perfectly acceptable initial system. Petty seems to have been clearly aware of the irreversible changes that had taken place in both the economic system and the apparatus of government. He also seems to have been aware that if the two had not been affected in the same way it was the apparatus of government that should be adapted to the level of development achieved in the economy. Thus, for example, in considering public offices (that is, positions assigned to private citizens at the pleasure of the sovereign, to provide public services remunerated, not from the public purse, but by charges levied directly on the users) Petty points out that these positions have multiplied because of the increasing complexity of society. At the same time that such activity had increased it had also taken on a *routine* character, so that much of the original justification for the high tariffs charged, achieved through the granting of positions of legal monopoly, had been eliminated: "Whereas at first such large Fees were allowed as

. . . should compensate the Art, Trust, and Industry of the Administratour; yet the large said fees are still continued, although the skill and trust be lessened, and the number of the said Fees so extreamly multiplyed. . . ."[5]

The fiscal system should above all be "just." This requirement is also derived from strictly economic reasons: the collection costs of a tax that is widely accepted are relatively low.[6] The equity criterion is illustrated as follows:

> Let the Tax be never so great, if it be proportionable unto all, then no man suffers the loss of any Riches by it. For men (as we have said but now) if the Estates of them all were either halfed or doubled, would in both cases remain equally rich. For they would each man have his former state, dignity and degree.[7]

In other words, the system should be constructed so as to leave the existing social structure unchanged. Petty believed that taxation, which in modern economies is often used to carry out redistributive policies, should be restricted to the sole objective of financing government expenditure. In this position Petty is doing no more than repeating a principle already stated by Hobbes: the State exists in order to guarantee the mutual respect of individual self-interests, as expressed in the existence of private property; the individual should thus contribute to the costs incurred by the State in fulfilling its functions in proportion to their wealth. On the other hand, Petty does not object to the existence of wide social disparities: "This equal spreading of Wealth would destroy all Splendor and Ornament . . . which would be to leave the face of Beggery upon the whole Nation: And withal such Parity would beget Anarchy and Confusion."[8] In any case, it was a question of an implacable law of nature: "That some are poorer than others, ever was and ever will be."[9]

According to Petty proportional taxation should apply to all types of income, including wages. Even if wages were close to subsistence, a reduction was considered possible and desirable.[10] In addition, Petty distinguished between "two sorts of Riches, one actual, and the other potential."[11] Proportional taxation should not be levied on either income or patrimony because they were both considered as "potential" wealth. Taxes on consumption, or excises, besides being "just," encouraged parsimony, avoided double taxation ("forasmuch as nothing can be spent but once"), and eased the gathering of statistics on the economic condition of the nation.[12]

Besides the criterion of equity, taxation should also be subject to other constraints. Considered to be the most essential were certainty over regulations, which should be simple, clear and evident (this would also keep conflict and judicial dispute, which were a waste of the society's resources, to a minimum); impartiality and a low cost of collection.[13] Other suggestions included the level of taxation and the terms of payment.

5.3 Petty does not furnish any precise criterion, but only some vague indications, for the question of the absolute amount of tax that should be collected each year by the State. His principal contribution on the subject concerns a concept which is now widely used by experts in the field of public finance, that of "fiscal pressure." Without ever using such a term, Petty frequently refers to the relation between the amount of taxation and the level of national income (or of consumption). It is in these terms, for example, that he presents his calculations on the required amount of taxation,[14] or the comparisons of the positions of different countries with which Petty intended to demonstrate that high taxes are not necessarily damaging (indeed, the country in which fiscal pressure was the highest, Holland, was also the richest[15]), but that a high level of public expenditure, in particular if it is connected with the maintenance of the King and his Court, is not necessarily an indication of great wealth in a country (the farce of the Court of the Sun King was not an indication of the greater wealth of the French, but of a higher level of fiscal pressure with respect to England).[16]

Naturally, a high level of fiscal pressure is only acceptable if the money collected is spent usefully, and in order to avoid tax receipts exceeding expenditures it would be necessary to be able to correctly predict the tax yield that would be produced by a particular set of fiscal regulations:

> if the Sovereign were sure to have what he wanted in due time, it were his own great dammage to draw away the money out of his Subject's hands, who by trade increase it, and to hoard it up in his own coffers, where 'tis of no use even to himself, but lyable to be begged or vainly expended.[17]

The scarcity of the available data concerning the economic system not only made calculation of receipts difficult, but also the determination of the most suitable method of payment, "for not knowing the Wealth of the people, the Prince knows not what they can bear; and for not knowing the Trade, he can make no Judgement of the proper season when to demand his Exhibitions."[18] The problem not only concerns the timing, but also the means of payment of taxation. For example, in an economic system where money is scarce, settling taxes in kind would be desirable. This would make it possible to avoid premature and costly forced sales, which make it especially burdensome for farmers to obtain money to pay taxes; it would also reduce the quantity of money necessary to the economy, thereby benefiting production.[19] The proper operation of the fiscal system would then require that the State have an adequate statistical service at its disposal. Petty put forward a number of specific proposals in this regard, in addition to proposals which we have already considered in other contexts, such as the land registry.[20]

5.4 Naturally, Petty qualifies the basic principles discussed in the preceeding paragraphs with a series of practical considerations. For example, the extreme simplicity and equity of the expenditure tax, obtained by taxing only final consumption expenditures and not their means of production, might at the same time greatly increase the difficulties of collection. It would thus be necessary to renounce proposals that were considered to be ideal from the theoretical point of view, but difficult to realize, in order to assure the creation of an efficient fiscal system, which would take empirical account of the various practical problems:

> the very perfect Idea of making a Leavy upon Consumptions, is to rate every particular Necessary, just when it is ripe for Consumption; that is to say, not to rate Corn until it be Bread, nor Wool until it be cloth, or rather until it be a very Garment; . . . But this being perhaps too labourious to be performed, we ought to enumerate a Catalogue of Commodities both native and artificial, such whereof accompts may be most easily taken, and can bear the Office marks either on themselves or on what contains them; being withall such, as are to be as near Comsumption as possible: And when we are to compute what further labour or charge is to be bestowed on each of them before consumption, that so an allowance be given accordingly.[21]

In addition, in contradiction with the principle of simplicity, which would have implied the choice of a unique tax on expenditure, Petty recommends the introduction of some particular taxes, such as fines to be levied on the followers of religious orders other than the State religion, and financial penalties for those guilty of minor crimes, which at the time were still punished by means of a variant of the law of retaliation: "an eye for an eye."[22]

Other taxes could be considered as representing payments for services rendered to the public. Customs duties, which may be supposed to have been originally introduced as payment for the protection offered by the Sovereign to those engaged in international trade, offer an example.[23] The level of duty actually charged was determined, however, by rather different considerations. For example, export duties were used by the State to appropriate any differential advantage that might be enjoyed by domestic producers with respect to their foreign competitors, allowing to home production only the minimum margin necessary to assure the competitivity of its own products. Even in such cases, however, it was necessary to take practical considerations into account: "the Measures of this Nature are, that it be more easie, safe and profitable for men to keep the Law, then to break it,"[24] an analogous principle to that proposed for the determination of the financial penalties for minor crimes.[25] Petty did, however, condemn customs duties within a Kingdom, and in particular those charged against Irish exports to England, without exception since they imposed useless and damaging obstacles to the expansion of productive and commercial activity.[26]

Petty's position is not quite so clear-cut in dealing with the problem of inflation, which is also considered as a particular kind of tax. The devaluation of the currency, in fact, "amounts to no more than a Tax, upon such people unto whom the State is indebted, or a defalkation of what is due; as also the like burthen upon all that live upon Pensions, established Rents, Annuities, Fees, Gratuities, &c."[27] The depreciation of money, which is produced by an increase in the proportion of base metals in the alloy mixed with the gold or silver in currency, had both positive and negative effects. On the one hand, for example, it made the export of money more difficult (the export of the precious metals was considered detrimental to the economy at that time), while on the other hand it made counterfeiting of the currency more profitable.

5.5 Among the general principles that Petty sets out, we have already discussed (section 5.3 above) the one which states that the total of taxes collected should not exceed public expenditure. Implicitly Petty also rejects the opposite condition, an excess of public expenditure over tax receipts. In an epoch in which financial intermediation was still in its earliest stages of development, the existence of a budget deficit (the country's budget was in fact considered identical to the King's personal balance sheet) could have grave political consequences resulting from the conditions that might be imposed on the Sovereign in exchange for loans to cover the deficit. Indeed, the francophile foreign policy of Kings Charles II and James II, which was subject to veiled criticisms from Petty in a number of his publications, can be explained, at least in part, by the financial conditions extracted by Louis XIV from the impoverished English Kings.[28] The objective of national independence on the one hand, and the necessity of minimizing the wasteful extraction of resources from its citizens on the other, justifies the hypothesis, implicit in all of Petty's analysis, of a balanced budget. Thus the problem of the utility of tax receipts is linked to the utility generated by the expenditures.

Given these premises, Petty can coherently state that taxes will not diminish the wealth of the nation because what is collected with one hand is put back into circulation with the other by means of public expenditure, given that the money collected is not destroyed or exported without producing any counterflow of imports.[29] At the same time some taxes, associated with specific forms of public expenditure, may directly contribute to the enrichment of a country if they encourage the movement of productive activity from sectors that produce goods destined for immediate consumption to sectors that produce durable goods (naturally the effect can also be negative if there is a transfer of activity in the opposite direction).[30] Nevertheless, tax-financed public activities, even if they are not directly productive, will be necessary to guarantee the orderly functioning of the productive sectors of the economy.[31] From this point of view it is only possible to recommend the elimination of excessive public expenditures, and Petty advances a number of proposals to this end.[32] It should be obvious that there is no substantial difference between this objective and that of reducing direct costs of production to a minimum.

But for Petty the duty of the State was not only to assure the provision of a limited number of institutional services. The direct intervention of the State in the economy by means of a policy of public works can produce an increase in wealth by increasing the level of production. In particular, by putting the unemployed to work producing goods that had been previously imported it would be possible to bring about an improvement in the trade balance.[33] The unemployed could even be put to work on completely unproductive projects, on the condition that this did not bring about an increase in imports.[34] These proposals are justified, not only by the increase in wealth that they could bring about, but also because they satisfy the exigence of maintaining the skills and efficiency of the available labor force, temporarily without employment in the directly productive sectors. This recommendation follows directly from Petty's consideration of the labor force as part of the national wealth.

In order to establish the limits to such policies of public works, Petty produces a series of calculations which attempt to determine "how much all the People could earn, if they were disposed, or necessitated to labour, and had Work whereupon to employ themselves; and compare that summ, with that of the total expence above mentioned." The potential full-employment income calculated in this way must then be compared with the actual income earned by labor which may be obtained by subtracting total nonlabor incomes, that is, rents and profits, from total income.[35] It can thus be clearly seen that Petty's position on government intervention in the economy is far ahead of his contemporaries and contains a number of original aspects which will eventually form the basis of the analysis of the problem found in modern economic theory.[36]

6

The State and
the Economic System

6.1 Money, international trade, and the fiscal system were already the subjects of everyday debate in Petty's time. What differentiates Petty's treatment of these subjects from that of his contemporaries and predecessors, beyond simple differences in the positions that he supports, is the method that he applies to analyze them. We have already discussed this method in chapter 2 where it was summarized in the catch phrases "political arithmetic" and "political anatomy." The object of Petty's analysis is the "body politick," that is, the State. He uses these two terms (while he never uses the term "economic system" which is much more common today) to convey the combined sense of the terms "political system" and "economic system." Thus, even if the economic aspects are given greater emphasis in his work the more strictly political considerations are never completely absent.[1] On the other hand, neither Petty, nor his contemporaries, felt the necessity to distinguish between the two aspects of what was considered a single line of enquiry. As is well known, the birth of capitalism was inherently linked to the birth of the nation-state. As Marx observed: "The concept of National wealth creeps into the work of the economists of the seventeenth century—continuing partly with those of the eighteenth—in the form of the notion that wealth is created only to enrich the state, and that its power is proportionate to this wealth."[2]

It is probable that Petty was acquainted with the work of Machiavelli[3] and a relationship between the contribution of the first to economic science and of the second to political science may be seen in the "systemic necessity" which we have already discussed in chapter 2. Machiavelli advances a unified conception of the nation-state, giving particular attention to the problem of the political unification of the city and the countryside. Petty, even when he is examining specific problems such as money or taxation, always reasons with reference to the "body politick" which is the object of the entirety of his research.[4] In both cases, the relations that are singled out of the complex network of social interdependences (economic and political) as being of greatest importance are those among the citizens of the same State, and between the Sovereign and his subjects. This represents a decision of double significance concerning the level of aggregate. A lower level of aggregation is rejected because the relations among the citizens of a single State, and between the Sovereign and his subjects, are considered as fundamental with respect, for example, to the relations between the inhabitants of the same village or between a Justice of the Peace (or any other local government official) and those who are under his jurisdiction. A higher level of aggregation is rejected because the system of international relations among citizens of the various States is considered as being subordinate to the interrelations among the States themselves. It is also rejected because it is not possible to attribute to such a system of relations a sufficient degree of stability and automatism, the prerequisites for the formulation of theoretical propositions which are intended to identify the uniformities that allow us to hypothesize laws of behavior for the system as a whole.[5]

6.2 The limits to Machiavelli's, and Petty's, conception should, however, be recognized. On the one hand is the fact "that Machiavelli should only have been able to express his programme and his tendency to relate city to countryside in military terms."[6] On the other hand, as we shall see more clearly in the discussion of the theory of prices in chapter 8, Petty uses a notion of the economic system that is not fully satisfactory. Such a conception would seem to be implicitly defined on the assumption that the network of relations and of exchanges which constitute the life of the productive system is subordinate to a unique political authority; but Petty does not recognize the other essential aspect of this phenomenon, that is, the fact that a unitary whole is necessary to give coherence to the complex system of relations among the various productive sectors, none of which could survive without the others.[7] Machiavelli does not perceive the interrelationships that exist between city and country, nor Petty the interrelationships between agriculture and industry, *from the point of view of production*. It is thus not surprising that Machiavelli discovers the relationships that link the two categories that make up the State, and Petty, those factors connecting the various sectors of the economic system, in the political superstructure. It is precisely the ability to go beyond this superficial point of view to discover the technological relations of production that link the various sectors of the economy, which constitutes the major contribution of the Physiocrats to the birth of economic science. It is in Quesnay's *Tableau Economique*[8] that the productive process is represented for the first time as a circular flow in which the outputs of each sector are used as either means of production in other sectors or as necessary means of consumption, while only a part of the total national product can be used for unproductive ends, such as luxury consumption. The same conception forms the basis of the theories of Ricardo, Marx, and Sraffa.

The fact that Machiavelli's and Petty's writings simply reflect the still extremely limited development of the productive forces at that period should not, however, be forgotten. The "industrial" activities that Petty launched on his Irish estates were, for example, vertically integrated. Any distinction between the various phases of the productive process, which extended from the production of raw materials to the fabrication of final product, or even between the manufacturing processes of production and the agricultural activities, which Petty attempted to develop simultaneously on his Irish properties, were of a purely bookkeeping nature.[9] In addition, particular changes in the political superstructure were indispensable to the passage from feudalism to capitalism, for example, institutions to guarantee private property in the means of production (in the first place of land: recall Petty's insistent support for the creation of a land registry, and in general the importance of a standardization of deeds for landed property).[10] It would thus be possible to interpret the conception of the economic system implicitly adopted by Petty, in the light of the conception of the State proposed by Machiavelli, as an expression of a particular phase of development of the economic system, that of the transition from feudalism to capitalism.[11] For each phase of development, the central object of the analysis for the economist is to be found at that level of aggregation that corresponds to the qualitative jump between economic integration and nonintegration: the hunting tribe, the agricultural village, the feudal castle with its surrounding land, the duchy and the principality with their city-country links, and finally the nation-state. Recognition of the historically determined limits to the significance of Petty's conception highlights the fact that no single definition of the economic system should be considered as an immutable law of nature. The process of expansion of the area of economic integration need not limit itself to the Nation-State, but tends to engulf the entirety of the area of capitalist development, overcoming the obstacles of customs barriers, producing the unification and standardization of juridical regulations applicable to economic relations, leading to an ever-increasing international economic integration (in terms of the international division of labor and the unification of national markets), as well as producing increasing influence on, and interference in, the formulation of internal economic policies of the various countries.

6.3 Having rapidly passed under examination the limits of the concept of the body politic utilized by Petty in his analysis, we can now turn to a review of the positive aspects, that is, to the elements of economic reality that such a concept allows us to clarify. Let us start by considering in more detail the general characteristics of the functioning of the economic system which emerge from Petty's analysis.

As the discussions of the preceding sections have already pointed out, the existence of an economic system as the area in which regular economic relations occur requires the existence of a framework of political and social support which guarantees the perpetuation of particular relations of production and of property. This support function is carried out by the apparatus of the State (the administrative and judicial branches) which thus plays a decisive role in guaranteeing the normal operation of economic activity. This is the object of Petty's analysis: implicit in the concept of the body politic is not only the directly productive apparatus, but also the apparatus providing the "support functions" necessary to guarantee and control the functioning of the former. Understandably, in a period of formation of the modern economic and political structure, it should be the relations between these two apparatus that occupies the center of the analysis. Thus, for example, Petty is more concerned with improvements in the organization of the fiscal and judicial apparatus, than with agricultural productivity.[12] The two aspects—directly productive activity and its necessary preconditions—are nevertheless continuously and explicitly connected. And if from one side the wastes associated with the survival of activities, inherited from the feudal period and no longer appropriate to the new productive reality, are widely condemned, on the other side Petty's work reveals a comprehension of the necessity of appropriate political structures and of the social utility of labor employed in this type of unproductive activity. It is precisely the central role played by such a link between the political superstructure and the economic structure in the period in which Petty lived (a link leading implicitly to the conclusion that the former should also be considered as an object of analysis by economists and included with the latter in the wider concept of the economic system) that justifies the identification of the limits of the economic system with that of the State, the basic unit of aggregation for the analysis of the political superstructure.

6.4 The problem of the relation between the political and institutional superstructure and the economic structure, between the preconditions of capitalist production and the production itself, can also be examined from the traditional viewpoint of the distinction between productive and unproductive labor. Before developing Petty's views on this point, and in order to get a better idea of his position within the context of the history of economic thought, it will be useful to quickly review the positions of the major writers on this issue.

Before Adam Smith, implicit or explicit definitions of productive labor were based on the distinctions between the various sectors, or the various products, and were connected with the various definitions of the concept of wealth. Thus, for the Mercantilists, it appeared that only (or above all) labor employed in foreign trade, which procured for the nation that which is considered as the single true wealth—gold and silver—was productive. For the Physiocrats only agricultural labor was productive or, more precisely, only land was productive, and as a corollary, agricultural activity was productive. At the same time Quesnay explicitly introduced the fundamental distinction between necessary labor (what Smith was to call useful labor) and productive labor: "if that which is productive is necessary, that does not imply . . . that all which is necessary is productive." [13]

With Smith (who continues, however, to give agriculture a priviledged position, presenting it as the *most* productive sector, even if it is not the *only* productive sector[14]) the distinction between productive and sterile sectors disappears and productive labor is defined as that which leads to the production of material goods. [15] Marx has discovered indications of a second definition in the *Wealth of Nations*, which identifies labor that produces income as productive. [16] Building on this definition, Marx shifts the emphasis of the discussion of the problem, and tends to identify productive labor in terms of the way production is organized. For Marx, as is well known, productive labor produces surplus value. That is, taking the viewpoint of the agent who organizes and regulates production (the capitalist), Marx defines as productive labor that which is productive from the point of view of the capitalist because it produces profit for him. This definition of productive labor is fundamental for Marxist analysis because it is the basis of the distinction within the social system of areas of capitalist production and all the rest (survivors from previous modes of production, the political superstructure, etc.,). Such distinction, together with the hypothesis that the social relations within the capitalist area dominate the system, organizing and utilizing the other areas of society for its own ends, is at the basis of the system of "specific abstractions" upon which the analysis of *Capital* rests.

6.5 It is not possible to find an explicit and unequivocal formulation of the problem of the distinction between productive and unproductive labor in Petty's work. As usual, Petty's theoretical conception has to be deduced from brief passages, and above all from the way in which he resolves the various practical questions which are the immediate objective of his writings. However, the various indications combine to form an extremely interesting whole.

In the forefront of Petty's ideas is the recognition of the relation between the productive structure and political superstructure and its services. As we have seen in section 6.3, a political and administrative connective tissue is necessary for the very existence of the economic system. The ensemble of functions that must be combined to constitute such a connective tissue is carried out by categories of labor which enter into what Smith in his *Wealth of Nations* defined as "useful" unproductive labor (lawyers, bureaucrats, for example; doctors and teachers, from this point of view, are included in the same category because they assure a given level of efficiency of the labor force).[17] Such activity, inasmuch as it is distinct from actual production, is in fact indispensable to those activities that are, directly productive of material goods.

Petty, who does not trace an explicit line of division between productive and unproductive labor, seems to include even such support activities in the category of productive labor to the extent to which they contribute to the production of wealth. Various passages in his work can be interpreted in this sense, including that in which he comes closest to a formal definition of productive labor: "the Wealth of the Publick will be diminished" if a tax produces a transfer of wealth from "labourious and ingenious Men" (Petty also includes soldiers and sailors in this category in that they procure gold, silver, and jewels for the kingdom) "to such as do nothing at all, but eat and drink, sing, play, and dance; nay to such as study the Metaphysicks, or other needless Speculation; or else employ themselves in any other way, which produce *no material thing, or things of real use and value in the Commonwealth.*"[18]

The only labor that Petty considers to be clearly unproductive is that which is in excess of the requirements of the system, which is particularly prevalent in the "political" and "administrative" apparatus in the wide sense. The excess of priests and lawyers is an example of this type of excess.[19] Indeed, in the early phases of the development of capitalism, these are the sectors in which the residuals of feudalism, the form of social organization about to be superseded, are most prevalent. Thus the significance of Petty's suggestions to eliminate labor in excess of that level strictly necessary (such as those favoring restricted entry into Universities and the redrawing of the boundaries of parishes)[20] can be better understood within the particular context of the transition from feudalism to capitalism. Petty's other suggestions, such as those relating to the institution of a land registry (cf. section 6.2, note 10), that represent real "technical progress" in the institutional superstructure by reducing its labor requirements, should be interpreted in the same sense.[21]

6.6 Petty establishes a ranking of the various sectors in terms of productivity: "There is much more to be gained by Manufacture than Husbandry, and by Merchandize than Manufacture."[22] This position might be considered as a form of residual mercantilism caused by Petty's imprecise definition of "productive labor," yet the criteria he introduces in drawing up the list have interesting theoretical implications. Petty follows two distinct criteria, both based on empirical considerations.

On one side he adopts the mercantilist criterion of foreign trade as a privileged sector because it favors the "production" of wealth *par excellence*, the precious metals. But this mercantilist position is not accepted absolutely, placing gold in one category and all goods in another. Rather it is justified on the basis of a criterion very similar to the definition of productive labor introduced by Adam Smith. According to Petty, a sector is more productive the more durable the output that it produces. There is then a ranking which starts with services and runs through food, clothing, housing and ends with the precious metals.

For example, speaking of the effect of the imposition of a tax accompanied by an expenditure of the same amount, Petty says:

> if Money be taken from him, who spendeth the same as aforesaid upon *eating* and *drinking*, or any other perishing Commodity, and the same transferr'd to one that bestoweth it on *Cloaths*; I say, that even in this case, the Commonwealth hath some little advantage; because *Cloaths* do not altogether perish so soon as *Meats* and *Drinks*: But if the same be spent in *Furniture of Houses*, the advantage is yet a little more; if in *Building of Houses*, yet more; if in improving of *Lands*, working of *Mines*, *Fishing*, &c. yet more; but most of all, in bringing *Gold* and *Silver* into the Country.[23]

In the absence of a clear distinction between consumption and investment, or a clear understanding of the central role of accumulation in the capitalist system, Petty determines his ranking within the group of goods destined to consumption in terms of their capacity to be, at some future moment, utilized for accumulation.[24] This ultimate use is not made explicit, and Petty seems to consider accumulation only under the form of the accumulation of private wealth, not of the accumulation of the means of production. Thus, the passage just cited continues by explaining why gold and silver are more attractive than any other good:

> Because those things are not only not perishable, but are esteemed for Wealth at all times, and every where: Whereas other Commodities which are perishable, or whose value depends upon the Fashion; or which are contingently scarce and plentiful, are wealth, but *pro hic et nunc*.[25]

We may be able to connect this affirmation to the level of development reached by the English economy, and in particular the example of the Dutch economy, founded on commerce, in the period in which Petty was writing. It is still the phase of mercantile capitalism, when the enormous private accumulations of wealth take place which are a necessary precondition for actual capital accumulation.

On the other hand, in order to establish the relative productivity of different types of labor, Petty falls back on the differences in wages of labor in different occupations. It is on this basis that agriculture is given the lowest position in the classification, and commercial activity (particularly in foreign trade) the highest.[26] A number of observations may be made on the significance of this classification. In the first place, Petty frequently uses wage differentials to support his first classification of the different sectors, that based on the durability of the products: but there is no *a priori* reason why the two classifications should coincide, and in fact there are some significant differences (for example, services). In the second place, (and Petty points this out, in particular in the case of sailors) wage differentials may be simple reflections of the differences in the qualification required for the different occupations. But, in this case one would have to explain why the sectors requiring more highly skilled labor are more productive than those sectors requiring unskilled labor. Putting the question from the point of view of the employer, is it possible to earn a higher rate of profit by employing skilled rather than unskilled labor? In the third place—and here we may find a justification for Petty's position—sectoral wage differences, as Smith would later point out, can also be explained by the different growth rates of the different sectors: a higher rate of growth requires a higher flow of labor from other sectors, and to induce this transfer the higher demand for labor must be accompanied by a higher level of wages, and vice versa for the declining sectors which are shedding labor. Among such sectors Petty notes in particular agriculture, which already at that time appears to have constituted a vast reserve of surplus labor power (a sign that the agricultural revolution was already under way).[27] In practice, those sectors that exhibited a significant amount of disguised unemployment were defined as "least productive," and those in expansion as "most productive." Given that Petty was living in the period of transition to capitalism, the classification that he drew up gave special weight to the sectors in expansion so that it corresponds, even if inexactly, to a classification of the sectors of the economy based on their potential within the emerging capitalist system.[28] But this is an interpretation "derived" from Petty's position, and if we want to remain within the limits of direct interpretation of his ideas we must be content with a notion of productivity essentially determined in relation to the accumulation of private wealth, considered as simple and undifferentiated power to command commodities and others' labor, and not as the material basis for a continuous expansion of productive capacity.

6.7 But even more important than the relative weight of the different sectors in the national economy in determining the wealth and power of the State is its population. This factor is at the center of Petty's interest, so much so that many consider him more a demographer than an economist. In fact, such a classification of Petty's work must be rejected since Petty only takes up questions of demography within the broader context of his study of the "political anatomy" of the functioning of the State which implies, as we have already seen, the study of the economic system. Besides, the problem of population is related to fundamental questions of economic analysis, such as the definition of wealth.

Petty confronts the problem of population by stating that he considers it "a mistake, that the greatness and glory of a Prince lyeth rather in the extent of his Territory, then in the number, art, and industry of his people, well united and governed."[29] Indeed, "People" are "the Naturall and true riches of his Kingdome."[30] Referring to a specific case, the scarcity of population in Ireland is that country's "greatest and most fundamental defect."[31]

A large population contributes to the wealth of a nation in two ways. In the first place, population itself constitutes a part of the national wealth, a part that can be evaluated quantitatively, just as other material goods such as land, houses or money. Petty frequently returns to this point, offering a number of estimates of the economic value of the population and the average value of each person.[32] In addition, even though its share in total national wealth is variable, it is nonetheless a relevant share and as such is often of decisive importance in determining the relative position of two countries.[33]

In the second place, an abundant population enriches a country more than in proportion to its actual size because of the advantages that may be derived from greater density. Petty here refers not only to the greater possibilities for division of labor and economic growth (which will be discussed more fully in chapter 7), but also, and more directly, to the possibilities of real economies of scale in the costs of the unproductive apparatus necessary to the proper functioning of the economic system (rulers and bureaucrats, judges, priests, soldiers, etc.):

> Fewness of people, is real poverty; and a Nation wherein are Eight Millions of people, are more then twice as rich as the same scope of Land wherein are but Four; For the same Governours which are the great charge, may serve near as well, for the greater, as the lesser number.[34]

In addition, a higher density of population augments not only the value of the population itself, it also increases the value of land.[35] Thus, among the objectives to be pursued by the Sovereign should be that of encouraging demographic expansion.[36] Petty offers several suggestions for policy in this direction, such as a program to increase the birthrate,[37] as well as his frequently repeated policy of *transplantation.*[38]

6.8 Petty considers every measure to increase the population favorably because he considers that it is "a false opinion, that our Country is fully peopled."[39] It is not clear, however, whether he considers increasing the population to be a process that should be carried forward without limit, or whether he considers that there is some "optimal level of population," greater than that in existence, but nevertheless finite.[40] Lansdowne, the editor of the *Petty Papers* and the *Petty-Southwell Correspondence*, supports the latter hypothesis, suggesting that the optimal limit will occur at the density that allows each man three acres of land, a formula that has also been used by the Reform Movement during the nineteenth century.[41] But it is evident that such a proportion can only have meaning within a given state of technology; the optimal density should increase with improvements in the methods of cultivation of land.[42] To have anticipated this slogan of a reform movement of some two centuries later cannot be considered as one of Petty's most important contributions. Among other things, the slogan "three acres per man" does not occur in any of his major writings, in contrast to his other political proposals which are usually clearly stated. It thus seems sensible to suppose that Petty, a man with a practical turn of the mind, was uniquely interested in the problem that was of direct relevance at the time, a population density that he considered to be insufficient given the prevailing conditions of agricultural technology, and that he was little aware or interested in how the problem might be resolved in the unknown conditions of the distant future. Further, when Petty discusses conditions in Holland, where the density of population is far superior to that which he (according to Lansdowne's interpretation) considered optimal, Petty expresses the opinion that the country is advantaged by the fact, and not impoverished by an excessive overpopulation.[43]

Petty also considered the grand urban agglomerations as highly beneficial. Part of the investigations he carried out in his later years was an attempt to demonstrate that London was the largest city in the world.[44] He implicitly considered this as an important positive factor in measuring the power of England relative to other countries.

Petty considers a number of advantages associated with the existences of large cities. They cover factors such as an improved administration of justice, a more efficient dispersion of technical knowledge with the attendant advantages for the production of output, and, especially, the reduced costs of transportation.[45] Petty also emphasizes the impact that the growth of a city has in increasing the value of the surrounding land, thus anticipating (as we shall see more clearly in the following chapter) the theory of differential rent based on the increase in the cost of transportation caused by an increase in the distance to be traveled to the nearest market. The only inconvenience of large cities of any importance that Petty considers is the possibility of an increased rate of mortality in the presence of epidemics.[46] But, on the whole, Petty is clear that large urban agglomerations are a decided advantage to the wealth of the kingdom.

It should not be necessary to point out in concluding the discussion, in this section and the preceding section, of Petty's views on the question of population (the positive benefits of an increase in population and the advantages of urbanization) that they clearly reflect the needs and the level of development of the society in which he was living and working.[47]

7

Surplus and Distribution

7.1 It has already been explained, in chapter 2, how Petty's concept of political anatomy, with the "body politick" as the basic objective of analysis, may be represented as reflecting a "systemic necessity." In the succeeding chapters, and especially in chapter 6, we have seen how that necessity could be translated into a conceptual framework which, even if partial and imperfect, permits the reasonably satisfactory identification of the role of certain economic categories (money, fiscal system, international trade, population, etc.) in the functioning of the economic system.

In this chapter, and the next, we shall make a closer examination of the potential, and the limits, inherent in Petty's approach for the construction of an analytical system capable of confronting the problems of the surplus, of prices and of distribution, that is, of the problems that would eventually come to constitute, after Petty's time in the golden age of classical economics, and which still constitute today, the nucleus of economic theory.

As we have already indicated, it is precisely on this point, and particularly in the theory of prices, that Petty's approach exhibits limits so serious as to make it possible to separate the treatment of these problems which can be seen to be inseparable within the framework of more advanced analyses. The quantitative measure of the surplus would, in fact, require a system of relative prices, which in its turn, given the competitive hypothesis of a tendency to a uniform rate of profit in the various sectors, would require knowledge of one of the distributive variables (wages or rate of profit) and of the technology, i.e., a physical representation of the surplus itself and of the way in which it is generated.[1] The absence from Petty's work of this essential connection between the surplus and distribution, represented by the theory of prices, allows us to separate the examination of his ideas on the concept of the surplus (which will be the subject of the present chapter) from the examination of his ideas concerning the measure of value and the relations of exchange (which will be the subject of chapter 8).

In fact, the identification of the concept of the surplus, even if in the partial form of rent, is traditionally considered as being one of Petty's most important contributions. Section 7.2 analyzes this claim. Section 7.3 will discuss the factors that Petty indicates as determining the size of the surplus, and in particular among these, his analysis of the division of labor. Midway between the problems of the surplus and the problem of distribution, section 7.4 examines the motives behind Petty's decision to exclude wages from the surplus and consider them as part of the necessary costs of production. Section 7.5 is then dedicated to the exposition of the elements of a theory of the rent of land offered by Petty's analysis. We will then give, in section 7.6 some brief reflections on the composition of the surplus, and changes over time in the proportions of the various sectors, concluding with an evaluation of the elements of Petty's analysis examined in this chapter.

7.2 As pointed out above, Petty clearly distinguished the concept of the economic surplus which would come to form the basis of all of classical political economy. But, for Petty, the surplus took the form of the rent of land and, by extension, the rent of money capital (interest):

> Suppose a man could with his own hands plant a certain scope of Land with Corn, that is, could Digg, or Plough, Harrow, Weed, Reap, Carry home, Thresh, and Winnow so much as the Husbandry of this Land requires; and had withal Seed wherewith to sowe the same. I say, that when this man hath subducted his seed out of the proceed of his Harvest, and also, what himself hath both eaten and given to others in exchange for Clothes, and other Natural necessaries; that the remainder of Corn is the natural and true Rent of the Land for that year; and the *medium* of seven years, or rather of so many years as makes up the Cycle, within which Dearths and Plenties make their revolution, doth give the ordinary Rent of the Land in Corn.[2]

It should be noted that the amount of rent is expressed here in physical terms, as a given amount of corn. This is possible because the product is homogeneous, while the heterogeneous means of production are all expressed in terms of the single produced good; this includes labor which is assumed to receive its means of subsistence, also expressed in terms of corn ("what himself hath both eaten and given to others in exchange for Clothes"). The problem of prices does not then exist, for it is implicitly assumed that the exchange ratios between the single produced good and the various means of production may be considered as given. The limitations of this formulation may be partially overcome by following a suggestion made by Petty himself to consider the sector which produces corn as comprehensive, covering all the productive activities necessary to assure the replacement of its necessary means of production: a "sub-system" as it would come to be called by Sraffa.[3] Petty makes use of such an instrument to establish the relative value of commodities, comparing the surplus quantities of each commodity produced by sub-systems which utilize the same quantities of labor:

> But a further, though collaterall question may be, how much English money this Corn or Rent is worth? I answer, so much as the money, which another single man can save, within the same time, over and above his expence, if he imployed himself wholly to produce and make it; *viz*. Let another man go travel into a Countrey where is Silver, there Dig it, Refine it, bring it to the same place where the other man planted his Corn; Coyne it, &c. the same person, all the while of his working for Silver, gathering also food for his necessary livelihood, and procuring himself covering, &c. I say, the Silver of the one, must be esteemed of equal value with the Corn of the other.[4]

The surplus can also be expressed in terms of the number of persons who can be maintained by a group of laborers who are producing the strict necessities they require for themselves and for the others. Just as the production of services and luxury goods, unemployment thus appears as a particular method of employing (or better, of wasting) the surplus:

> if there be 1000. men in a Territory, and if 100. of these can raise necessary food and raiment for the whole 1000. If 200. more make as much commodities, as other Nations will give either their commodities or money for, and if 400. more be employed in the ornaments, pleasure, and magnificence of the whole; if there be 200. Governours, Divines, Lawyers, Physicians, Merchants, and Retailers, making in all 900. the question is, since there is food enough for this supernumerary 100. also, how they should come by it? whether by begging, or by stealing . . . ?[5]

The proposals for public works, as pointed out in chapter 5, section 5, were intended precisely to transform potential income, which is nonetheless a part of the surplus, into effective income, i.e., a larger quantity of produced output.[6]

Given that Petty conceived of both output and means of production in terms of labor, it should have been easy for him to take the additional step forward to achieve an expression of the surplus in terms of excess labor, i.e., as the difference between the number of hours that labor is normally required to work and the working time necessary for them to reproduce their own means of subsistence. According to Marx, Petty did in fact take this step in the passage quoted at the beginning of this section,[7] but in reality, although Petty does come very close to the Marxian conception—closer here than in any other place—it does not seem possible to accept Marx's claim that he clearly formulates such a position.

In the same way, once the surplus is expressed as the difference between output and means of production composed of different quantities of the same good or expressed in terms of labor, calculation of the "rate of surplus" should have been straightforward. It should also have then been simple to conceive of the rate of profit as a ratio between the surplus obtained in production and the aggregate of the means of production advanced. But notwithstanding the widespread use of the analogous concept of the rate of interest, already well known at the time, and the comparisons made by Petty between the rate of interest and the yield of land,[8] the concept of the rate of profit does not appear in his analysis, nor does Petty encounter any analytical problem that requires comparison of the surplus obtained with the amount of capital anticipated.

It should be remembered, on the other hand, that in the age in which Petty was writing, the relations of production which lay beneath the analysis of the surplus were primarily relations between landowners and agricultural laborers, so that the form in which the surplus normally presented itself was in the form of rent. In a similar way we can explain the relatively scarce attention attributed to the problem of the surplus relative to that of the formation of wealth (this point of view also emphasizes the extent to which Petty may be considered as much more "modern" than his predecessors and contemporaries). In the phase of original accumulation, capital is formed by the private appropriation of social wealth—think of the experience of Petty himself in Ireland. It is thus understandable that the attention of students of such problems in that epoch should have been concentrated on wealth. Once this initial phase of accumulation is superseded, capital is accumulated essentially by means of private appropriation, on the part of the capitalists, of the surplus (as would occur in the golden age of classical political economy, when in fact it was common to argue that the rate of growth of the system depended on the rate of profit).

7.3 In relation to the question of the determinants of the magnitude of the surplus, Petty anticipates the basic arguments of Smith in the *Wealth of Nations*, emphasizing the number of productive laborers and the level of productivity per worker. These two elements are referred to jointly, for example, in the explanation of the greater wealth of the Dutch.[9] In relation to the first of these two factors, we again refer to Petty's insistence on advancing propositions that he aimed to provide employment for the greatest possible number of productive laborers, either by engaging unemployed workers or by transferring labor from unproductive activities, as well as the quantitative importance he attached to such proposals, in terms of the potential increase in income and wealth which could be thus produced.[10]

It will be the scope of this section to give a more detailed analysis of the second element, productivity per worker. Petty points out that among those factors influencing productivity there are some, which may be called "natural," which should not be overlooked. These include the ease of access to the sea, the availability of harbors and natural avenues of communication, and even the "natural" fertility of the land.[11] But, Petty attaches much greater importance to technological and organizational factors which, after the completion of the initial phase of development of a colony or any other undeveloped territory, are linked to the social evolution of the different peoples who inhabit them.[12] Among such factors Petty singles out improvements of the land (drainage, irrigation, etc.) and investments in infrastructure (roads and navigable canals),[13] emphasizing the importance of technical progress embodied in new implements of production.[14] Finally, particular importance is given to the division of labor. It will be helpful to our understanding of Petty's position on this important point to consider more closely the two passages where he sets out his arguments most clearly. In *Political Arithmetick* (written between 1671 and 1676, but published posthumously by his son in 1690) Petty says:

> Those who have the command of the Sea Trade, may Work at easier Freight with more profit, than others at greater: for as Cloth must be cheaper made, when one Cards, another Spins, another Weaves, another Draws, another Dresses, another Presses and Packs; than when all the Operations above-mentioned, were clumsily performed by the same hand; so those who command the Trade of Shipping, can build . . . a particular sort of Vessels for each particular Trade.[15]

Several years later, in *Another Essay in Political Arithmetick*, published in 1682, Petty returns to the argument, proposing another example, watches:

> in so vast a City . . . each *Manufacture* will be divided into as many parts as possible, whereby the Work of each *Artisan* will be simple and easie; As for Example. In the making of a *Watch*, if one Man shall make the *Wheels*, another the *Spring*, another shall Engrave the *Dial-plate*, and another shall make the *Cases*, then the *Watch* will be better and cheaper, than if the whole Work be put upon any one Man.[16]

The division of labor is a recurrent theme in Petty's writings treating the economic and social questions of his time. In his *History of Economic Analysis* Schumpeter speaks of the question as "this eternal commonplace of economics," noting that Plato in his *Republic* had described the phenomenon "with unusual care,"[17] and Marx in his *Capital* refers in this regard to Plato, Xenophon, Isocrates, and Diodorus Siculus.[18] But, in the passage reported above it is possible to identify a number of elements of extreme interest in Petty's position on the problem. In the first place we should note that he highlights not only the division between the different sectors of production and the territorial division of labor,[19] but also the division of tasks among the different laborers within the same productive activity. In the second place, as Marx would later note, Petty, "views the *social* division of labour only from the standpoint of *manufacture*, and sees in it only the means of producing more commodities with a given quantity of labour, and, consequently, of cheapening commodities and hurrying on the accumulation of capital. In most striking contrast with this accentuation of *quantity* and *exchange-value*, is the attitude of the writers of classical antiquity, who hold exclusively by *quality* and *use-value*."[20] Finally, we note how in his explanation of the Dutch domination of international trade the reduction in costs due to the division of labor and the expansion of the market due to the reduction in costs are considered to interact in the process of economic growth.

This last point was taken up a few years after the publication of Petty's works by the anonymous author of the *Considerations on the East-India Trade* (1701), who also adopts Petty's examples, reported above, of the fabrication of clothes, ships, and watches.[21] This writer, as well as others of the same period (Harris, Locke, and Mandeville, for example) may be considered as a bridge between Petty's early work and Smith's later *Wealth of Nations* which has become the traditional reference for the classical position on the division of labor. It is true that

Smith never cites Petty's works, but then neither did he cite the *Ency-clopedie* from which he borrowed his celebrated example of pin-making.[22] The fact remains that for this argument, as for many others, Smith simply adopts and expounds in a systematic way ideas that had already found fragmentary expression in the writings of his predecessors,[23] among whom, in a more or less direct line, Petty must be considered as one of the most important sources. On the other hand, even Marx, who made considerable contributions to the discussion of the subject by relating the different forms of the division of labor to the different phases of economic and social development, explicitly refers to Petty's work on a number of different occasions and reproduces Petty's watch example in great detail.[24]

In conclusion we can say that even if Petty did not offer an explicit treatment of the division of labor, the examples that he provides demonstrate that he had clearly understood the nature and the importance of the concept. In the same way as Smith, but considerably before him, Petty grasps this central element of the manufacturing phase of capitalist development. Although from the modern reader's point of view Petty's treatment has obvious limits in his failure to identify the interrelationship between the division of labor and the growth of mechanization and large-scale industry, this can be better understood by recalling the extremely limited development of capitalism in the age in which he lived.

7.4 As we have already pointed out, Petty does not consider wages as a part of the surplus. Following an already firmly established tradition, which would endure until the time of Ricardo and Marx, Petty considers wages as fixed at the level of subsistence (to be understood in the historical and not the biological sense)[25] but, differently from his successors, he views this as an objective that is to be pursued by means of the formulation of laws to regulate maximum wages, rather than as the result of autonomous natural forces such as the Malthusian law of population:

> the price of labour must be certain, (as we see it made by the Statutes which limit the day wages of several work men;) the non-observance of which Laws, and the not adapting them to the change of times, is by the way very dangerous, and confusive to all endeavours of bettering the Trade of the Nation.[26]

Petty's position is thus rather different, not only from the position which, after Malthus, would come to be generally accepted by the

Classical economists,[27] but also from an analogous thesis that had already been put forward by Mun in one of his well-known writings, *England's Treasure by Forraign Trade*, published posthumously in 1664 and the center of much subsequent debate:

> Neither are these heavy Contributions so hurtful to the happinesse of the People, as they are commonly esteemed, for as the food and rayment of the poor is made dear by Excise, so doth the price of their labour rise in proportion.[28]

Mun does not give an analysis to justify his statement. Petty, on the other hand, considers the level of wages to be determined by law, even when they are above the subsistence minimum, and he limits himself to clarifying the consequences of such a situation:

> then the Law that appoints such Wages were ill made, which should allow the Labourer but just wherewithall to live; for if you allow double, then he works but half so much as he could have done, and otherwise would; which is a loss to the Publick of the fruit of so much labour.[29]

In other words, if the hourly wage is fixed by law at a level that is too high, the number of hours worked would diminish until the point was reached where total earnings had returned to the level of minimum subsistence. Differently from Mun, Petty bases his position on a precise hypothesis concerning the behavior of the working classes which described what Petty considered to be common knowledge.[30] Petty's objective in the case of legislation on wages, as for other questions, is always to increase the power and the wealth of the kingdom. In this particular case, the achievement of that objective required that the quantity of labor supplied by a given number of workers should be as high as possible. On the other hand, these "workers" do not appear to be included in Petty's definition of the "public" which, in the passage quoted above, are supposed to benefit from the "fruits of labor." Petty does not recognize any moral problem in suggesting that wages be reduced to the minimum level strictly necessary for subsistence. Unlike Mun, who demonstrates a certain sympathy for the "poor," and considers the fact that taxes should ultimately fall on the "rich" as an acceptable consequence,[31] Petty condemns such "fallacious tenderness towards the poor" who are not adequately taxed,[32] emphatically declares that social inequality is a fact of nature,[33] and warns that "such Parity (of income) would beget Anarchy and Confusion."[34]

Petty's position combines certain traditional views, remnants from forms of social organization that are already or are about to become outmoded, as well as hints of a more modern nature produced by an unprejudiced understanding of the nature of the new relations of production which were in the process of being established. On one side we have the references to social inequality as a fact of nature, which brings to mind the Platonic conception of a society rigidly structured in distinct sectors determined according to the function carried out, or the feudal society which was still widespread in Europe and even in England in Petty's time. On the other side it is evident that the recommendations, such as those recorded above, are based on a method of argument designed to support a particular objective, the maximization of labor time, which was essential for the success of the new mode of production. We could say that Petty confronts the problem from the point of view of the active participants in the political and economic society of his time, from the point of view of those who organize production and participate in the distribution of the surplus. Although the surplus could be increased by means of improvements in the state of technology and in the organization of labor (not only within each single branch of productive activity, but also in the society considered as an integrated whole), it was also possible to increase it by reducing the expenditure on the labor force, considered as the means of production of the system which could be both produced and reproduced. Petty considered the labor force as a commodity similar to any other commodity. Thus its costs of production had to be reduced to its minimum level in order to produce the maximum possible surplus, which was considered as the basic objective of society—but of a society in which the laboring classes were not included.

7.5 We have already seen how Petty identified the surplus with the rent from land, which he defined as the difference between the value of output and the value of the means of production, and whose magnitude was determined by the same factors (productivity and wages) as determined the surplus. Petty also makes some more specific observations concerning rent; in particular he demonstrates consciousness of the existence of differential rent based on differences in the fertility of the different types of land:

> the goodness or badness, or the value of Land, depends upon the greater or lesser share of the product given for it in proportion to the simple labour bestowed to raise the said product.[35]

In addition, he clearly identifies the existence of a differential rent based on the relative distances from the market of different plots of land and thus on the relative differences in the costs of transport of their produce:

> doth great need of Corn raise the price of that likewise, and consequently of the Rent of the Land that bears Corn, and lastly of the Land it self; as for example, if the Corn which feedeth *London*, or any Army, be brought forthy miles thither, then the Corn growing within a mile of *London*, or the quarters of such Army, shall have added unto its natural price, so much as the charge of bringing it thirty nine miles doth amount unto.[36]

In this passage Petty states that rent is determined by the price of the product, following a line of reasoning that brings to mind Ricardo's argument that an increase in the price of corn would be the result of bringing less and less fertile land into cultivation.[37] But this argument is given within the framework of a theory of absolute rent and Petty does not recognize the possibility, which would later be exploited by Ricardo, of eliminating rent from the price of the product by concentrating on the conditions of production on marginal land. As a result of this incomplete analytical development of the problem, a number of inconsistencies emerge in Petty's treatment of the impact of taxation on the rent of land. In some cases (when the landowners are not constrained by long-term rental contracts) taxes can increase rent gross of the tax, thereby increasing the price of the product.[38] Petty forgets to point out, however, that this result is only possible if the increase in the price of agricultural products does not bring about a subsequent increase in nominal wages, and thus an increase in the prices of all other goods. Since the level of rent gross of taxes can only increase if the total surplus, with which it is identified, is also increased, Petty's statement will hold only if costs of production, and specifically real wages, decrease.

7.6 The growth of rent, as a result of the identification of rent with the surplus, thus coincides with the growth of the economic system as a whole. But, side by side with agricultural production, the other sectors of production will be expanding even more rapidly. For this reason, distinguishing rent from other forms of appropriation of the surplus leads to the result that rent should diminish as a proportion of national income in the process of expansion of the economy. At the same time, landowners should lose their position of absolute predominance in society. Petty recognizes this latter tendency, but his identification of rent with the surplus leads him to represent this process simply as a reduction in the importance of land among the various costs of production:

> that this accumulating of operations & Labor and art upon the first and most simple product of the Earth, doth diminish the value of the Land. That is, makes it to beare a far less proportion to the labor bestowed upon it than formerly, when raw wheate or wheate onely boyld or parched did satisfy men's appetites.[39]

The argument is reversed in conditions of an increasing density of population. In this case rent would tend to increase in absolute terms during the process of economic growth. Petty does not fail to point out that the same results would be produced by his proposal to transport the Irish population to England.[40]

All things considered, Petty does not limit his consideration of the process of economic growth to a purely quantitative phenomenon (the growth of the size of the surplus), but also recognizes the qualitative transformation of the productive structure of the economy which makes itself perceptible moment by moment in terms of the differences in wages and profitability in the various sectors of the economy.[41] At the same time, however, this correct intuitive conception of the qualitative nature of the process of development is not translated into a systematic exposition of the phenomenon because of the grave analytical limits to Petty's investigations. This failure may be traced, in particular, to the identification of the surplus with rent alone, in which Petty also included interest on money, but omitting the incomes of artisanal labor and, above all, profits. We shall return to this problem in the next chapter, but in the present context we should observe that in the initial phases of capitalist development, in which the structural transformations are the most profound, the typically capitalistic categories of income—wages and profits—have not yet assumed any precisely identifiable autonomous role. This fact may help us to understand why, in Petty's times, the theory of the surplus, and of its distribution, could not yet be formulated in the Classical manner of a confrontation between the rate of profit and the rate of wages, supposed uniform in all branches of economic activity.

8

The Problem of Prices:
From a Conceptual Position
to Analytical Difficulties

8.1 The last subject that we must deal with is the evaluation of Petty's contribution to what is generally considered to be the central problem of political economy: the relations of exchange of commodities, i.e., the problem of relative prices. From a number of points of view Petty's position on this question must be considered as a fundamental contribution to the birth of economic science. This may be seen, above all, at the all important level of the formation of the basic concepts of economic analysis. This problem, which is generally ignored by economists, in fact constitutes a necessary precondition for any analytical investigation. Indeed, theoretical concepts such as "commodity" or "market" or "natural price," which are accepted as if they were inherent to economic analysis, are in reality the result of a conscious process of abstraction. And the way in which this process takes place, with the various modifications that it implies for even the content of an analytical concept, has profound implications for the very point of departure of any analytical inquiry.

Petty directly confronts such problems as they concern the definition of the concepts of commodity, market, and natural price, even if he does not discuss the problem in modern terminology. Petty's contribution to this crucial problem is presented in section 8.2, dealing with the concepts of commodity and market, and in section 8.3, dealing with the concept of price. We will then be in a position to examine, in section 8.4, the way in which Petty confronts the problem of relative prices, by attempting to trace a unique interpretative theme through the various seemingly self-contradictory positions proposed by Petty in his writings. These run from the seeming adoption of a theory of labor value, to a more complex theory of land-and-labor value, and finally, to a more general framework based on "physical costs." Within the framework thus established it will be possible, in section 8.5, to undertake an evaluation of the solutions that Petty proposed to the problem of establishing an equivalence between the two central elements of his theory of value, land, and labor. In section 8.6 the further developments of this position by Cantillon and others will be evaluated. We will then be in a position to make an assessment of Petty's contribution, attempting to identify the subsequent lines of development of the theory of prices which may be traced back to Petty's work.

8.2 Our investigation of Petty's contribution to the problem of the formation of the concepts of commodity and market starts with consideration of a few pages of a short essay which takes the form of a conversation: *The Dialogue of Diamonds*, unpublished until 1899 when Hull included it in his edition of Petty's economic writings.[1]

The protagonists of the dialogue are Mr. A, representing Petty himself, and Mr. B, an inexperienced buyer of a diamond. The latter sees the act of exchange as a chance occurrence, a direct encounter producing a conflictual relationship between buyer and seller, rather than a routine episode in an interconnected network of relationships, each contributing to establish stable behavioral regularities. Mr. B, who has no norm which might allow him to establish a unique reference point for the correct price of diamonds, thus considers the exchange as an inherently risky act. As such, it would be impossible for him to take precautions so as not to be cheated in what is a unique event, the bargaining with the seller who he presumes to have a more extensive knowledge of the market.[2] He might seek the advice of a friend who is more expert. But this would not help unless the friend possessed some specific rules of thumb which could be used to determine the proper price.[3] The problem is, in fact, a difficult one because any specific individual diamond, even if it may be considered as belonging to a single category of marketable good, differs from every other diamond on account of a series of quantitative and qualitative characteristics, as well as the particular circumstances (time and place) of its sale.

Neither Mr. A nor Mr. B explicitly mention the relationship between the development of a regular market on the one hand and the possibility of defining any given category of goods (the set of the various individual diamonds) as a commodity ("diamond" in general) on the other. This possibility is in turn necessary for the derivation of the abstract notion of theoretical price (the "natural price" of a "diamond") from the multiplicity of actual exchange relationships. There is, nevertheless, a crucial relationship between the way an economic system functions and the possibility of extracting significant abstract categories capable of providing a theoretical representation of reality.[4] In the absence of a market where routine exchange occurs, the characteristics and circumstances of differentiation mentioned above operate in such a way as to make each act of exchange a unique episode. The price is subject to wide and erratic fluctuation, and the relative bargaining abilities of the buyer and the seller play a significant role in its determination.

On the other hand, the existence of a regular market, large enough to even out the extreme fluctuations, allows the transformation of those elements which differentiate individual acts of exchange from one another into homogeneous differences in price. Mr. A, the expert, is in fact aware of the existence of precise quantitative relationships between the prices of the different types of diamond determined by weight, dimension, color, and defects. After explaining the manner in which each element is quantitatively assessed through the determination of grading scales for the qualitative elements, he then goes on to explain how each single one of them, and then their combinations, affects prices (given the choice of the price of a particular type of diamond as a standard of reference, a problem which will occupy us in the following pages). Thus, for example, "The general rule concerning weight is this that the price rises in duplicate proportion of the weight."[5] A similar rule applies to the dimension. The average of the prices obtained on the basis of these two rules determines the "political price" as given by both weight and dimension.[6] This will be the price for a diamond without defects and with good color. Adjustment coefficients would have to be applied to determine the price of diamonds exhibiting defects and unsatisfactory coloration. The scales for both of these coefficients are supplied by the market.[7] Naturally, the blind application of these rules to determine diamond prices may lead, on occasion, to absurd results whose correction will require the application of adjustments determined by experience as well as simple common sense. For example, at the conclusion of the Dialogue, Mr. B observes that the rigid application of the rules may in some cases (in particular when a single diamond contains a number of different defects) lead to negative prices. Mr. A. grants the validity of the criticism and suggests some possible corrections which should avoid such difficulties.[8]

Taken as a whole, Petty's writings offer a satisfactory representation of the process of abstraction required for the formulation of the concepts of "market" and "commodity" from the multiple particular exchanges that occur in the economy. This generally favorable judgment on Petty's work is subject to two qualifications, however.

First, in the case of diamonds analyzed by Petty, the process of abstraction producing the commodity "diamond" from the myriad of individual stones, each differing one from the other in its specific characteristics, is directly related to their physical attributes. This is a very different type of abstraction from that implicit, for instance, in the Marxian concept of "abstract labor." A diamond, among other things, is a commodity whose price is determined more by scarcity with respect to demand than by its cost of production. It is thus exchanged in a market that is isolated from other markets, for it has no productive interrelationships with the commodities traded in any other market.

Second, Petty only implicitly specifies the analytical consequences of the fact that the market is itself an abstraction. This point deserves further investigation which can be achieved most easily by reference to some remarks that occur in *The Dialogue of Diamonds*.

As we have just stated, the market is an abstraction in the sense that each individual act of exchange concerns a specific diamond, exchanged at a specific time and place, at a specific price (Mr. B, the inexperienced buyer is right). The relationships that Mr. A, the expert, sets up between the various subcategories of the goods exchanged and prices are not, as Petty himself observes (and as we shall see more clearly in section 8.3), deterministic in any absolute sense, for they can be "modified" by any number of contingent circumstances. The market exists as a concept which is useful, indeed indispensable, to an understanding of the functioning of an economic system, only to the extent that it is possible to abstract from the myriad of individual exchanges a given set of relationships which can be considered as representative of actual experience and which provide a guide to behavior. The same considerations apply to the concept of the commodity. In fact, reality is composed of an infinite number of specific individual objects. It is the economist who groups them into categories, such as "diamonds," according to particular characteristics which are considered to be most important, ignoring other characteristics judged to be of lesser importance.

In other words, the commodity cannot be considered as the basic element of economic reality, for it is itself an abstraction which is formulated on the basis of a deliberate decision concerning the level of aggregation necessary for its definition. This level of aggregation is determined by the scope of the analysis and by the extent of the interrelationships between the various exchanges. In the present case, diamonds can be considered as a commodity having a specific market because the links among the various individual exchanges of particular diamonds are such as to make the hypothesis that they are one and the same good acceptable. Thus the differences in weight, dimension, and color may be reduced (as Petty proposes) to quantitative differences which can be expressed by means of a scale of predetermined coefficients which are independent of prices. In other cases, different basic units might be chosen for the analysis, such as "pear market," or "fruit market," or more generally "food market." Then the decision as to whether "pear," "fruit" or "food" is chosen as the commodity is determined by the level of aggregation thought to be most relevant. It is evident that the determination of the existence of a market (that is, the meaningfulness of the hypothesis that a certain set of exchanges may be considered as subject to uniform general conditions) depends not only on the relationships established in the market, but also on the basis of those exhibited by the category of individuals classed as producers and the category defined as buyers.[9]

8.3 Abstraction is also necessary in formulating the concept of price, which is necessary to the resolution of the analytical problem of the determination of relative prices. The reason for this is not only that the concept "price" is always associated with a "commodity" and as such is also a single-valued representation of a multiplicity of values corresponding to the specific individual goods grouped together to form (as we have seen above) a single category of commodity; it is also useful, in the face of continual variations in prices in time and space, to appeal in the course of analysis to a particular standard or reference price.

This is the path that Petty follows, distinguishing between actual price and political price. It is the latter which corresponds to the natural price of the Classical economists, i.e., the theoretical price determined on the basis of an analytical scheme which is based on the forces acting on prices in a systematic way, ignoring the random elements. This distinction corresponds, as we shall see below, to the distinction between intrinsic causes determining the political price, and extrinsic causes, those variable and contingent causes which combine with the former to determine actual price.

Petty confronts this problem directly in a passage in *A Treatise of Taxes and Contributions* as well as in *The Dialogue of Diamonds*. In the *Treatise* Petty introduces three definitions which distinguish different concepts of price corresponding to different levels of abstraction in the analysis: natural price, political price, and current price. The first depends on the state of technological knowledge and on the required subsistence for the workers. The second also takes social costs, such as hidden unemployment, into account. Petty considers these costs as waste, given the fact that their existence implies that actual production is lower than potential production. Finally, current price is defined as the expression of political price in terms of the commodity used as the standard of measure. The passage in which Petty develops these definitions is rather long but is sufficiently important to be reproduced in full:

> . . . natural dearness and cheapness depends upon the few or more hands requisite to necessaries of Nature: As Corn is cheaper where one man produces Corn for ten, than where he can do the like but for six; and withall, according as the Climate disposes men to a necessity of spending more or less. But political Cheapness depends upon the paucity of Supernumerary Interlopers into any Trade over and above all that are necessary, *viz*. Corn will be twice as dear where are two hundred Husbandmen to do the same work which an hundred could perform: the proportion thereof being compounded with the proportion of superfluous expence, (*viz*. if to the cause of dearness abovementioned be added to the double Expence to what is necessary) then the natural price will appear quadrupled; and this quadruple Price is the true Political Price computed upon naturall grounds. And this again proportioned to the common artificiall Standard Silver gives what was sought; that is, the true Price Currant.[10]

Petty's "natural price" thus has the meaning of a target, or of an optimal price, a meaning which would later disappear in the use of the term by the economists of the Classical school. In Petty's writings it is the price corresponding to the best technology available (at least in principle) on the basis of the state of technology, and corresponding to the most efficient possible operation of the "body politick." In fact, the Classical idea of "natural price" corresponds to Petty's "political price," which regulates the behavior of the market and depends on the actual conditions of production prevailing in the economic system (Marx would subsequently refer to these conditions with the expression "socially necessary labor").[11] It would appear that Petty distinguished between these two concepts, in an historical period that was predominately one of transition from feudalism to capitalism rather than fully developed capitalism, in order to emphasize the higher costs attached to the then still backward level of social organization. It should be noted that the current price which is mentioned in the passage quoted above is itself a theoretical variable since it is simply the political price expressed in terms of money. On the other hand, it is clear that there are a number of other elements which act to determine the actual price at which exchange takes place in the marketplace:

> But forasmuch as almost all commodities have their substitutes or succedanea, and that almost all uses may be answered several ways; and for that novelty, surprize, example of superiors, and opinion of unexaminable effects do adde or take away from the price of things, we must add these contingent causes to the permanent causes abovementioned, in the judicious foresight and computation whereof lies the excellency of a merchant.[12]

Petty returns to the distinction between political price and actual price in *The Dialogue of Diamonds* where he singles out two groups of factors affecting the price of diamonds: intrinsic factors and extrinsic, or contingent factors. The former determine the political price (i.e., the theoretical price) while the latter explain the divergence of actual price from the political price. Extrinsic factors correspond to the casual circumstances of the specific acts of exchange, so that it is difficult to define them and apply to them precise rules for their reduction to homogeneous, comparable magnitudes. Intrinsic factors, on the other hand, are identifiable with precision, and it is possible to translate them in terms of price differences according to well-defined rules which may be determined by observation of (the averages) of the exchanges that actually occur in the marketplace (as Petty himself does in the case of the weight, dimension, quality, and defects of diamonds). In *The Dialogue of Diamonds* Mr. A, the market expert, illustrates the point in the following way:

> The deerness or cheapness of diamonds depends upon two causes, one intrinsec which lyes within the stone it self and the other extrinsec and contingent, such as are 1. prohibitions to seek for them in the countrys from whence they come. 2. When merchants can lay out their money in India to more profit upon other commoditys and therefore doe not bring them. 3. When they are bought upon feare of warr to be a subsistence for exiled and obnoxious persons. 4. they are deer neer the marriage of some great prince, where great numbers of persons are to put themselves into splendid appearances, for any of theise causes if they be very strong upon any part of the world they operate upon the whole, for if the price of diamonds should considerably rise in Persia, it shal also rise perceivably in England, for the great merchants of jewels all the world over doe know one another, doe correspond and are partners in most of the considerable pieces and doe use great confederacys and intrigues in the buying and selling of them.[13]

Of particular interest is the conclusion of the passage where Petty describes a worldwide market and stresses the fact that contingent events taking place in any part of the world could have an impact on any other part because the various particular (local) markets for diamonds are integrated in a single, unified world market ("the great merchants of jewels all the world over doe know one another"). On the other hand, it may cause surprise to see the prohibitions mentioned above included among the contingent elements, for they are institutional elements, and as such one might expect that they should be included with those elements that determine the political price. Nevertheless it should not be forgotten that Petty, who had pretensions of influencing royal decisions, tended to consider certain institutional obstacles to the development of exchange, and of the economy as a whole, as being capable of elimination. This applied particularly to restrictions on foreign trade.[14] As we have stressed above, the theoretical distinction between natural prices and political prices, just as a number of Petty's concepts, should always be interpreted in light of the practical intentions of the author, which was mainly to emphasize the detriment caused by institutional elements to the expansion of the wealth of England. Abstracting from this issue we are thus left with a separation between natural prices and political prices on the one hand and actual prices on the other. Petty bases his analysis on this separation, which clearly anticipates the Classical distinction between natural and actual, or market, prices.[15]

8.4 Having established the role of the concepts of commodity, market, and political price in the preceding sections we are now in a position to investigate Petty's analysis of relative prices.

A number of different interpretations of Petty's position on relative prices already exist. The first, put forward by Marx, and adopted by a number of Marxian historians of economic thought, credits Petty with a more or less fully developed and coherent labor theory of value.[16] Indeed, there are a number of passages in Petty's writings which appear to support this interpretation. For example, in *A Treatise of Taxes and Contributions* we find:

> let a hundred men work ten years upon Corn, and the same number of men, the same time, upon silver; I say, that the neat proceed of the silver is the price of the whole neat proceed of Corn, and like parts of the one, the price of like parts of the other.[17]

And a little further in the same work Petty states:

Natural dearness and cheapness depends upon the few or more hands requisite to necessaries of Nature: As Corn is cheaper where one man produces Corn for ten, then where he can do the like but for six; and withall, according as the Climate disposes men to a necessity of spending more or less.[18]

Even more explicit than these passages, however, is Petty's proposal of what appears to be a theory of value based on labor and land:

All things ought to be valued by two natural denominations, which is land and labour; that is, we ought to say, a ship or garment is worth such a measure of land, with such another measure of labour; forasmuch as both ships and garments were the creatures of lands and mens labours thereupon.[19]

This passage also raises an additional problem. Just as the quotations given above, it is intended to provide an explanation of exchange relationships. Yet, the reference to "natural denominations" suggests that it might also be interpreted as a rudimentary statement of a theory of absolute value.[20] The following formula which Petty uses to state his theory of value lends itself to the same interpretation: "labour is the father and active principle of wealth, as lands are the mother."[21] This is a traditional slogan and was widely used by economists of the period. When we consider the diverse roles of labor and land in the agricultural process of production, the former playing the active, the latter the passive role, an idea which can be traced back as far as the writings of Aristotle, it is easy to see how such an idea might provide the basis for a theory of labor value grounded in the doctrine of "natural law."

In the scholastic tradition, which was still widespread in the seventeenth century, it was commonplace to identify the "just" price with that which enabled the producer to recover his costs and to obtain something in compensation for his work and effort. Some authors reduced all costs to labor costs, and went so far as to propose proportionality between the just price and the labor contained in commodities.[22] In the context of this type of interpretation, labor is conceived of as a *sacrifice* made by the producer. The price is thus the "just" reward for this sacrifice because, being proportional to the labor contained, it is also proportional to the sacrifice endured. Theories of labor value of this type implicitly contain substantial elements of subjectivism and often serve as an apology for the capitalist system. One has only to think of the justification of the subsistence minimum wage as the laborer's just recompense for the "sweat of thy face,"[23] and of the further developments by Senior, who discovered an equivalent sacrifice in the "abstinence" of the capitalist which received its "just" return in the form of profits.[24]

A full investigation of the evidence suggests, however, that such a "natural law" interpretation of Petty's theory of value would be erroneous. In fact, he considers labor as simply another production cost which is measured by its subsistence[25] and ignores any possible moral implication of justice or injustice in his treatment of the problem of prices. Indeed, this is his practice, on methodological principle, in all of his analysis. Furthermore, in Petty's view, land and labor should be placed on the same footing and he expresses either one equally in terms of the other. In fact, "the most important consideration in Political Oeconomies" is precisely, "how to make a par and equation between lands and labour, so as to express the value of any thing by either alone."[26] In the next section we shall return to the problem of the equation linking land and labor. Here it is sufficient to notice that it is clear and evident from the context of these statements that Petty is not working within a framework of "just" price nor does he rely on a "natural law" explanation of prices; rather he is seeking to explain the actual exchange relationships which are taking place every day in the market-place by means of the concept of "political prices." It should thus be clear that Petty did not consider labor and land as the "original" sources of wealth, but quite simply as physical costs of production of commodities.[27]

This interpretation of Petty's theory of price as being based on physical costs of production is not contradicted by passages, such as those reported above, which seem to support a labor theory of value. Indeed, given the fact that these statements are made within the context of a work in which the theory of value based on labor *and* land is explicitly set out, and in which the problem of the equivalence between land and labor is a central subject of discussion, one is instead led to the conclusion that these passages should be interpreted as a simplification with respect to a more complex theory based on labor and land, and that Petty is implicitly presuming the hypothesis of proportionality between the quantities of land and the quantities of labor used in the production of the various commodities. Moreover, there are passages in Petty's works in which he goes beyond the theory of value based on land and labor, moving farther along the path of physical costs of production. In fact, he even provides a list of the activities necessary to specific processes of production:

> The price of a commodity subsist:
> Of the first naturall materiall.
> The manufacture to the state of use.
> Carriage from the place of making to that of use, and vessels.
> Dutyes to the Soverayne to them that buy and sell.[28]

Petty mentions a series of examples of this principle, specifying the cost in terms of physical goods. Following this path, he also provides a correct formulation of the problem of joint production. Consider the first of the fourteen examples that Petty gives:

> *For butter*. There is 1. The cow. 2. Her feeding in winter and somer. 3. The dairy vessells and labor. 4. Carriage. Deducting: 1. Calf 2. Wheyes 3. Coarse cheeses.[29]

We can therefore conclude that Petty's analysis is primarily concerned with the problem of the determination of relative prices. Those statements that have been interpreted as attempts to formulate a theory of absolute value are in fact only intended to provide a basis for an analysis of exchange relationships. Petty's use of physical costs of production[30] gave an objective formulation to the analysis, a formulation which was to be followed by, among others, Ricardo, and in more recent times, Sraffa who provides a more systematic approach based on a higher degree of analytical rigor.

8.5 It is evident that Petty's contribution does not go much beyond the simple formulation of the problem: physical costs of production are the factors that determine political prices, which leaves the problem as far from resolved. Heterogeneous goods such as the cow, the feed, the labor, cannot all be summed together to make up the costs of production unless they have been previously expressed in homogeneous units, that is, in terms of quantities of value obtained by multiplying the quantity of each commodity required in the process of production by its relative price. We thus confront the problem of circularity. The price of the product cannot be determined unless the prices of the means of production are known, but since these are also produced by means of production, their prices can only be determined if the prices of their means of production are known, and so forth (think for example of the case of wheat used to produce iron which is itself used in the production of wheat).

Petty appears to be oblivious to this problem. Yet, it is precisely this difficulty which would account for his attempt to reduce the heterogeneous components of the costs of production to the two primary factors, land and labor, as well as the necessity of discovering a relation of equivalence between them which would allow costs to be expressed in terms of one single unit. But Petty's attempts were not successful, especially the latter, to which Petty attached the greatest importance. Consider the method that Petty suggests for establishing a relation of equivalence between land and labor:

> Suppose two acres of pasture-land inclosed, and put thereinto a wean'd calf, which I suppose in twelve months will become 1C. heavier in eatable flesh; then 1C. weight of such flesh, which I suppose fifty days food, and the interest of the value of the calf, is the value or years rent of the land. But if a mans labour . . . for a year can make the said land to yield more than sixty days food of the same, or of any other kind, then that overplus of days food is the wages of the man; both being expressed by the number of days of food.[31]

Petty immediately recognizes, and himself attempts to resolve, the most obvious problems such as the heterogeneity of the levels of consumption for different individuals and the heterogeneity of consumption goods:

> That some men will eat more than others, is not material, since by a days food we understand 1/100 part of what 100 of all sorts and sizes will eat, so as to live, labour, and generate. And that a days food of one sort, may require more labour to produce, than another sort, is also not material, since we understand the easiest-gotten food of the respective countries of the world.[32]

A similar criterion to that suggested to determine the equivalence between land and labor is also applied by Petty to the problem of reducing the "art," i.e., the skilled labor of an inventor to terms of simple labor:

> By the same way we must make a par and equation between art and simple labour; for if by such simple labour I could dig and prepare for seed a hundred Acres in a thousand days; suppose then, I spend a hundred days in studying a more compendious Way, and in contriving Tools for the same purpose; but in all that hundred days dig nothing, but in the remaining nine hundred days I dig two hundred Acres of Ground; then I say, that the said Art which cost but one hundred days Invention is worth one Mans labour for ever; because the new Art, and one Man, perform'd as much as two Men could have done without it.[33]

In fact, the solution Petty suggests is that which is now better known under the name of *efficiency units*. Land is compared to labor, and complex labor is compared to simple labor, by means of a comparison of relative productivity of the two elements in each case. But, this comparison required the prior knowledge of relative prices, and thus is also subject to the problems associated with circular reasoning. Alternatively, the problem could be resolved by measuring productivity in physical terms, but this would require that the outputs compared be homogeneous (which Petty attempted to do by reference to "daily food"). The latter alternative, however, implies the use of the unrealistic assumption of a "one-commodity world," and is therefore as unacceptable as the former solution. What is lacking in Petty's attempts to resolve the problem of the determination of relative prices is a perception of the simple fact that the problem is integrally related to the operation of the economic system as a whole and not to a single productive sector of the economy. The incompleteness of the conceptual scheme set out by Petty, and in particular the failure to recognize the crucial importance of a concept such as the rate of profit, appears to prevent a correct statement of the problem, much less its resolution by means of an analytical system which recognizes the interrelationships between the various productive sectors of the economy. But, the path that leads to such a system stretches a great distance from Petty's initial steps along it.

8.6. The first economist to continue along this path, shortly after Petty, was Cantillon who fully accepted the basic thesis:

> The Price and Intrinsic Value of a Thing in general is the measure
> of the Land and Labour which enter into its Production.[34]

On the other hand, Cantillon criticized Petty's proposed criterion for the equation relating land and labor as "fanciful and remote from natural laws":

> he has attached himself not to causes and principles but only to
> effects, as Mr. Locke, Mr Davenant and all the other English authors
> who have written on this subject have done after him.[35]

In other words, Cantillon correctly recognizes what we have discovered to be Petty's error: the attempt to base the comparison on the relative productivity (the "effects") of processes that alternatively use either land or labor. The alternative criterion which Cantillon proposes is, in effect, more consistent with the objective framework of the theory of prices: labor is reduced to its cost of production. In the words of Cantillon: "the daily labour of the meanest slave corresponds in value to double the produce of the land required to maintain him."[36] In fact, in addition to the maintenance of labor it is necessary to add an equivalent cost for the maintenance of two children in order to assure, given the mortality conditions of the period, the substitution of the laborer at the end of his active working life.[37] In other words, Cantillon considers a self-sufficient fragment of a self-replacing economic system. The surplus of this subsystem can be expressed either in terms of a quantity of labor expended in the period, or alternatively, as that quantity of subsistence goods that assures the availability of the laborer during the period and his "replacement" at the end of the period. In this way it is possible to state that a certain quantity of labor equals a certain quantity of "the produce of land." But, in reality such goods are not only produced by the land, but by all the other means of production existing at the beginning of the period, including labor. In any event, more than the problem of the determination of the relations of exchange (which are in effect assumed to be given), Cantillon seems to be trying to resolve the problem of the cause of value. From this point of view, the directions in which Cantillon moves, that is, that of reducing labor to its costs of production (to which Petty too had referred, as we have already seen, when he says that "the days food of an adult Man, at a Medium, and not the days labour, is the common measure of Value"[38]), might lead to a pure theory of land value, for land would be the unique, nonreproducible, original factor creating value.

Within the framework of an absolute theory of value of this type (exclusively attributing to land the capacity of *creating* value), and without explicitly raising the problem of the relations of exchange, which are once again assumed to be given data, the Physiocrats, and foremost among them Quesnay, were the first to recognize that the existence of heterogeneous means of production raised the problem of the productive interrelationships between the various productive sectors. But this problem, as it is confronted in the *Tableau Economique*, is only considered in terms of the exchanges necessary to assure the regular functioning of the economic system.[39]

In his *Wealth of Nations* Smith shifts the focus of the problem from land to productive labor. But, in terms of the problem of the relations of exchange his theory of "labor commanded" could not provide a solution for it only involves the choice of a specific unit of measure. An effective attempt to resolve the problem is, on the other hand, undertaken in Smith's attempt to reduce price to its component parts of wages, profit, and rent.[40] But even such a solution, which Sraffa baptized the "adding-up theory,"[41] is not acceptable. Ricardo, in particular, criticized Smith's tendency to ignore the interdependence that exists between the distributive variables: the rate of profit and the rate of wages.[42] Smith does, however, take another step along the path of a "systemic" vision of the theory of prices, placing the interdependence that dominates the price system, from the point of view of the market, at the center of his attention; translating it into an analytical hypothesis of the tendency of the rate of profit to uniformity in all the sectors of production. His authority has contributed to making this hypothesis into a fundamental element of the theory of prices and with which the labor value theorists would later encounter difficulties.[43]

Ricardo moved in an opposite direction from Cantillon and the Physiocrats, although he retained the framework of an objective conception of prices. Utilizing the Malthusian theory of differential rent, he could eliminate land from the analysis by considering only the technology on marginal land. This permitted Ricardo, in his *Essay on the Influence of a low Price of Corn on the Profits of Stock* (1815) to resolve the problem of distribution in a very simple manner within the context of a "one basic commodity model." If we are in an economic system that utilizes only wheat as means of production and as a means of subsistence for the labor employed in the production of wheat, we can immediately see that with an increase in the ratio of wages in output (caused in Ricardo's analysis by a reduction in output due to bringing less fertile land into cultivation while the wage remains fixed at subsistence) the rate of profit (given by the ratio of profit to capital advanced)[44] will be reduced. In this way the distribution problem is resolved without the necessity of confronting the problem of relative prices since all quantities entering the determination of the profit rate are expressed in homogeneous terms as different quantities of the unique good existing in the "agricultural" production process.

On the level of formal coherence Ricardo's reasoning is watertight, but it depends decisively on the assumption of a "one basic commodity world." Malthus immediately recognized this weak point in Ricardo's analysis and frequently pointed out in his correspondence with his friend and adversary that in reality workers do not consume only wheat, and that the means of production even in agriculture are multiple and heterogeneous with respect to the output they produce.[45]

Thus, in his *On the Principles of Political Economy and Taxation*[46] Ricardo is forced to confront the problem of prices as the logical premise to any theory of distribution. Once more, in order to keep the two problems distinct he attempted to find a solution to the first problem that was independent of the second, that is, to formulate a theory of the relations of exchange in terms that do not depend on the values assumed by the distributive variables. We have already noted that Ricardo, moving in an opposite direction from Cantillon and the Physiocrats, succeeded in bypassing the problem of land, leaving only labor as the unique "original factor." It is on this basis that he adopts the assumption, already well known amongst economists, of proportionality between the price of a good and the quantity of labor directly or indirectly necessary to its production.[47] But, as Ricardo himself points out, the theory of embodied labor cannot give a rigorous explanation of prices. In fact, the various quantities of labor directly or indirectly employed in the production of a good cannot be considered as homogeneous because they differ one from the other in terms of the time at which they are required in the process of production, and require a different charge for profit according to the length of the period that elapses between the application of labor and the moment the final product is completed. This is not the place to reproduce the entire history of the attempts to resolve this problem. It is sufficient to point out that these very same difficulties are at the center of the controversy concerning the "transformation of labor-values into prices of production" which has been debated, after Marx, by generations of supporters and critics of Marxism.[48]

More recently the problem of relative prices has been confronted by Sraffa[49] within the context of an analytical system that takes the interrelations in production among the various sectors into account as the link that joins prices and the distribution of income. Without entering into the arguments concerning the relevance of his solution, which at present constitutes the last word in the theoretical debate on the problem, we shall only point out that this solution is also achieved within the objective framework based on the physical costs of production. The characteristic distinction of such a conception is that prices are determined on the basis of technology, i.e., by the complex of the costs of production of the various commodities; that such costs are viewed as a complex of physical costs, i.e., as the quantities of means of production and of labor that in a given social and technological situation are necessary to obtain a given quantity of product; and finally that labor is seen, not as a sacrifice, but as an expenditure of human energy which is reconstituted by means of wage goods, thus permitting labor to be considered on the same analytical level as the other physical costs of production.

At the end of the journey we thus discover the very same conception of the problem of prices that is implicit in the work of Petty, although at a decidedly higher analytical level. The decisive progress that has been made in terms of the construction of an analytical system that furnishes an overall framework of the economic sytem, and which takes the interdependencies that link the various productive sectors into account, has also made it possible to add precision to this conception, which still remains as a constant basis in a line of thought that has developed over three centuries.

9

Evaluation and Conclusions

9.1 The conclusions reached in the preceding chapter concerning the theory of prices can be generalized to serve as a basis for an overall evaluation of Petty's contribution to the birth of political economy. As we have seen, Petty's work exhibits the great merit of having developed, either explicitly or implicitly, some of the essential categories of the modern theory of prices. These include both the concepts of market and commodity, as well as the distinction between current price and political price. In addition, Petty deserves recognition for having conducted his discussion of the problem of prices within a conceptual framework that would subsequently be adopted by a series of later writers from Ricardo to Sraffa. At the same time, Petty did not succeed in formulating a coherent analytical system capable of capturing fully the interrelationships that link the various sectors of the economic system to one another. Certain concepts that express these interrelationships, such as the rate of profit, are in fact absent from his analysis.

A similar judgment may be made of Petty's contributions to other branches of political economy which have been the subject of particular consideration in the preceding chapters. But, as the wide variety of the arguments that came under discussion demonstrated, the specific significance of each, considered case by case, diverges from this general judgment. For example, with reference to the subject of method considered in chapter 2, we observed that by choosing the scientific study of the "body politick" as his basic objective, Petty expressed the necessity of a systematic analysis of economic and social phenomena. Even if this necessity is not in fact translated into concrete results, Petty's methodological position appears to be correctly defined. The examination of Petty's opinions on money, international trade, and the fiscal system, (in chapters 3, 4, and 5), subjects which were among those most discussed by men of affairs and men of state in that epoch, furnishes a confirmation of the extent to which Petty contributed to the evolution of the framework in which economic research was carried out. It also demonstrates the new concepts and the expansion of analysis made possible within the new framework.

We have also been able to reconstruct Petty's ideas concerning the economic system as a whole on the basis of sparse hints scattered here and there in his various works. It was thus possible to judge Petty's systematic representation of the "body politick" with reference to various analytical questions, that of unproductive labor among them, and to conclude that it was sufficiently well articulated to allow a coherent discussion of these questions. Petty's contribution to the problem of analysis in the strict sense, on the other hand, is more limited. We saw in chapter 7 that although the concept of the surplus is clearly defined in Petty's work, it was identified with rent, and further that the distinction between the distributive categories (wages, profits, and rent) which was to provide the basis of the analysis of distribution in the golden age of the Classical economists and after is only vaguely recognized, if not completely absent (as regards profits). As we have seen in chapter 8, the absence of this distinction makes it difficult if not impossible to produce an analysis of relative prices.

9.2 On this basis we can attempt to give a response to the question that the historians of economic thought frequently pose with reference to Petty: founder of political economy or simple forerunner? An answer, formed on the basis of the analysis of the preceding chapters is not clear-cut for we have discovered strengths and weaknesses, fundamental contributions and basic deficiencies, intermingled throughout Petty's work. On the other hand, neither is it possible to identify a precise dividing line marking the limit of prescientific reflections on social and economic life and the application of political economy proper.

We should be careful, however, not to attempt to resolve dilemmas of this sort in a peremptory and definitive fashion, judging the past on the basis of more modern analytical developments, and above all on logical and conceptual schemes currently popular. As we have already pointed out in the introduction, this would lead to the identification of the beginnings of political economy with the first manifestations of liberalism if we approached the question from the viewpoint of someone ~e Smith or McCulloch, or with the first introduction of marginal calcula ion in economic analysis by adopting the viewpoint of someone like the young J.R. Hicks[1] or, from the Marxian point of view with the first statement of the labor theory of value. These assessments obviously would not reflect the history of economic thought, but would be a part of the theoretical debate itself. To expand and clarify this point, it is instructive to consider Marx's assessment with regard to Petty's contribution.

It is well known that the first published version of Marx's *Theories of Surplus Value* opens with the consideration of Petty's work.[2] But, it is also well known that this edition was prepared by Karl Kautsky who himself organized in chronological order the writers discussed in Marx's notebooks. The official edition prepared by the Marx-Engels-Lenin Institute in Moscow reproduces more faithfully the order of the original manuscripts which demonstrates that the material should be considered as an integral part of *Capital*. In this edition the discussion of Petty follows consideration of the Physiocrats and Smith.[3] Certainly, Marx speaks of Petty with great praise, as we have had occasion to witness in the quotations given above. He was even of the opinion that Petty should be attributed a central role in the birth of economic science. But we have also seen that Marx bases his judgment on an interpretation of Petty's work (the identification of the concept of the surplus and the first intuitions of the labor theory of value) which can only be considered partially correct.[4]

Nevertheless, there are a number of good reasons to support Marx's judgment that Petty was the "founder of Political Economy." In particular, if we accept the thesis that "every science constitutes itself . . . by means of a *leap* that surpasses empirical perception: the *act of conceptualization*. It is this leap, this epistemological rupture, which marks the beginning of every science."[5] We have in fact seen that Petty's contribution to the construction of the conceptual system adopted by political economy is substantial, and in some respects, decisive.

On the other hand, if we were to base our judgment on Petty's strictly analytical contribution, the result would undoubtedly be to consider Petty among the precursors of political economy. Even his most important contribution in this respect, the definition of the concept of the surplus, is in fact presented in the confused form of rent, while his analysis of exchange relations was far from systematic, representing little more than an initial consideration of the problem.

Faced with the substantial difficulties surrounding an unequivocal evaluation of Petty's work, it seems that the dichotomous judgment—founder, in the sense of the formulation of concepts, and precursor for what concerns systematic analysis—is far more useful to an understanding of the nature of Petty's contribution to economic science, and as a reasonably accurate indication of his position in the history of economic thought.

9.3 This judgment does not however exhaust the task we have set for ourselves in this book. As has already been indicated in the Introduction, the principal objective was not that of arriving at a judgment within the context of the history of economic thought in the strict sense (even if it is obvious that the understanding of the thought of an author requires that the conditions of the period in which he lived should be kept continuously in mind), but that of furnishing the instruments necessary to provide a deeper understanding of political economy and of its current lines of development.

From this point of view, a return to the sources of political economy allows us to recognize the interrelationships that exist between the phase of development achieved by the economic system on one hand, and the formation of the required analytical concepts and the development of proper economic analysis on the other. We have discussed both of these questions in a number of places in the previous pages, indicating some concrete examples of this interrelationship. But, rather than recalling our prior discussion of specific examples, we shall only reemphasize here two results of more general significance, often explicitly recognized, but just as often completely ignored in the current economic debate.

First, that every theory, every analytical system, is based on a series of concepts which combine to form an integrated overall conception of economic reality. It is for this reason that fundamental misunderstandings are possible in theoretical debate on questions, which at first sight appear to be based on analytical differences in the strict sense, if the conceptual framework in which the discussion is carried out is not kept clearly in mind.

Second, that political economy is a historical science by its very nature inasmuch as it attempts to understand a reality that is in continual evolution. Thus the very conceptual system that furnishes the basis for the theoretical constructions used to interpret that reality will itself evolve over time. Even those changes that might appear as improvements within an already existing conceptual framework (such as the introduction of the category of the general rate of profit in a representation of the economic system already based on the category of the surplus) should, at least in part, be considered as representing modifications that have also occurred in the structure of the economic system itself.

The study of the thought of an author such as Petty, who lived in the special phase in the development of capitalism associated with primary accumulation, can be particularly instructive for an appreciation of the importance of these two general principles. It also encourages a more accurate recognition of the implications of the conceptual system that is adopted, often without further reflection, by most contemporary economists in their theoretical research.[6]

Notes

Chapter 1

1. The standard biography of Petty is still that written by one of his descendents, Lord Edmond Fitzmaurice (1895). In addition to this source the contents of this chapter are based on the more recent biography by E. Strauss (1954), on the information furnished in C. Hull (1963), and by H. Lansdowne, cf. W. Petty (1927, 1927a), on the *Petty-Southwell Correspondence* edited by Lansdowne, cf. Petty (1928), as well as on the brief biography written by a friend of Petty's, J. Aubrey (1813). For the reception given Petty's work, see section 1.6.

2. W.L. Bevan (1894, pp. 393–94) suggests that Petty had adopted an invention of Sir Christopher Wren which he had the occasion to see at a stage when it had not yet been perfected.

3. Petty is one of those cases, rather common in the period, of a medical doctor who extended his interests from human anatomy to political anatomy. The most famous case is that of Quesnay, physician to the Court of Louis XIV, whose economic ideas (the *Tableau Economique*) were most probably influenced by Harvey's discovery, at the beginning of the seventeenth century, of the circulation of the blood in the body.

4. The professor of "music" at Gresham College was in fact free to occupy himself with any subject that might have a vague connection with "harmony," including the numerical expression of natural laws. The atmosphere of Gresham College, the operative center of the new scientific and empirical culture designed to seek the solution to practical problems, also encouraged such endeavors. Cf. C. Hill (1972).

5. W. Petty (1963, p. 149).

6. The forced transfer of a great mass of the population was not considered absurd in Petty's time. In Ireland itself there had been *plantations* in King's County and Queen's County in 1555, and in Ulster in 1603. Petty himself often proposed schemes of *transplantation*, cf. for example W. Petty (1963, pp. 157–58, 55lff.) and (1927, pp. 256, 261, 265–66). He adopted the same position with reference to slavery, accepting it as a natural fact, cf. Petty (1963, pp. 68–69), (1927a, pp. 21, 231). Petty even compares laborers to slaves, cf. Petty (1963, pp. 68–69, 152), (1927, p. 267). All this suggests that a certain prudence is necessary in attributing to Petty reservations of a moral nature against the programs of *transplantation*.

7. Just as the *Grosse Survey* seems to have been so named because of the "gross," or rough and ready, procedures employed, the *Civil Survey* was so called because it was meant to involve civilians rather than soldiers, and the *Down Survey* was due to the fact that the results were marked down on a map.

8. Petty's theoretical position on the division of labor is discussed more fully in chapter 7, section 3.

9. From the top of Mount Mangerton, which lay within his property in 1661, Petty could see 50,000 acres of his holdings. Cf. J. Aubrey (1813, p. 484).

10. Cf. W. Petty (1927, pp. 73–111, section IV, "Irish Land Registry") and *A Treatise of Ireland* (1963, pp. 570, 573). For similar propositions made with reference to England see, for example, *Political Arithmetick* (1963, pp. 264–65). The argument is discussed in chapter 6.

11. It is probable that Petty was more inclined towards the Cromwellians than the Monarchists, but a complete lack of scruple in such matters characterized Petty's political activity. A follower of Hobbes' political theories, Petty favored central authority, whoever might exercise it. After having been linked to Henry Cromwell, Oliver Cromwell's son and the Lord Lieutenent of Ireland, Petty was able to bring himself to establish good relations with Charles II and his Court.

A similar lack of scruple is displayed by Petty in his analysis of religious matters. For example, in one of his writings (reproduced in Matsukawa, 1977, pp. 48–50), Petty states that "Popery seems to me not a Matter of Religion but Policy," and goes on to compare the economic damages attributable to Ireland's leaning to the Church of Rome, rather than the Church of England, in terms of the greater number of holidays, priests, and so forth of the former.

12. Cf., for example, W. Petty (1963, pp. 141, 153–54, 601ff., 620).

13. From 1659 to 1666 Petty was normally resident in London, even though he was elected a member of the new Irish parliament in 1661. In 1666 he moved his residence to Dublin to follow more closely the work of the Court of the Innocents. He returned to London from 1673 to 1675 while he was trying to gain the right of collecting the Irish taxes. He returned to Dublin from 1676 to 1681 where he filled the position of Justice of the Admiralty, but made numerous trips to London where he reestablished himself from 1682–1683, only to go back to Dublin from 1683–1685. He passed the last years of his life, 1685–87, in London.

14. The story is due to J. Aubrey (1813, p. 486).

15. Cf. C. Hill (1972).

16. K. Marx (1941, pp. 82–84).

17. See section 1.6, or for a more complete documentation G. Keynes (1971). Lansdowne, in his Preface to Petty (1927), states that an enormous quantity of unpublished manuscripts are still in the possession of his family. The *Petty Papers* (1927, 1927a) as well as the *Petty-Southwell Correspondence* (1928) represent a selection from this material.

18. John Graunt (London, 1620–1674), man of commerce, highly appreciated by his contemporaries for his qualities as a mediator, was one of Petty's closest friends. As we have seen, he was instrumental in Petty's transfer from the chair of anatomy in Oxford to the chair of music at Gresham College. Petty returned the favor, supporting Graunt's election to the Royal Society in 1662. The *Observations* were an important factor in the success of Graunt's membership proposal, and this is the source of the hypothesis that Petty had "lent" the work to his friend in order to ease his election. Section 1.6 reviews some of the bibliographical evidence relevant to the discussion of the paternity of the *Observations*.

The fire of London in 1666 left Graunt at the edge of bankruptcy and his conversion to Catholicism contributed to his isolation. His refusal of Petty's offer to bring him to Ireland and his attempt to restore his own fortune in London created ever greater difficulties. He died on April 18, 1674 and Petty followed the funeral procession in tears. Further particulars of Graunt's life may be found in C. Hull (1963, pp. xxxiv–xxxviii).

19. See, for example, Petty's statements in the Preface to *A Treatise of Taxes and Contributions* (1963, p. 5). But this was not only an amusing distraction. Often it is the case of memoranda and short notes that Petty wrote to clarify his ideas on current problems in order to be in a position to put forward his own proposals and to be able to criticize those of others at the proper moment.

20. Among Petty's various proposals, in addition to that of the land register, which has already been referred to, there are a number that have only been adopted in recent times, such as the introduction of identity cards (1927a, pp. 204, 212) or of a national health service (Ibid., p. 175) or the substitution of a decimal system for the complex

English system of pounds, shillings, and pence, see *Quantulumcumque on Money* (1963, p. 447) and Petty (1927, p. 271). Others bear testimony to the fertility and eclecticism of Petty's genius, such as the proposal to use wool in the construction of fortifications (1927a, pp. 79ff.) or to construct "War Chariots," which Lansdowne considers as the forerunners of today's tanks (Ibid., pp. 61ff.).

21. See some of the writings collected in Petty (1927, pp. 116ff.) and in (1927a, p. 4) that deal with the themes of religion and logic. Frequent references to the education of his children are also found in Petty (1928).

22. Cf. Petty's letter to his wife cited in Fitzmaurice (1865, p. 160).

23. In Dublin, in 1684, Petty founded the *Dublin Philosophical Society* on the model of the Royal Society and became the first president (cf. Petty, 1927, pp. 87–92), but when Petty returned to London in 1685 the society became dormant and was eventually dissolved in 1687, the year Petty died.

24. Among Petty's manuscripts, to which Lansdowne refers (Petty, 1927, p. 253), there is one bearing the title *Matters in Transaction and Discourse since King James the Second his Coronation* which consists of a list of some forty different proposals that he put forward in the first months of the reign of the new Sovereign. Petty also prepared drafts of the order for his own nomination as *Accountant General*, a new position that he had suggested to the King. This proposal had no more success than any of the others.

25. On July 9, 1687, when the book had only just been published, Petty wrote to Southwell: "Poor Mr. Newton. I have not met with one person that put an extraordinary value on his book. . . ." A few days later, on July 23, he places a monetary value, as was his habit of mind, on his estimation of the value of the book: "As for Mr. Newton's book, I would give 500 £ to have been the author of it, and 200 £ that Charles understood it" (Petty, 1928, p. 279).

26. Petty (1963).

27. C. Hull (1963).

28. Petty (1927, 1927a).

29. Petty (1928).

30. Petty (1972).

31. Petty (1905).

32. G. Keynes (1971).

33. J.R. McCulloch (1953a).

34. W.L. Bevan (1894).

35. H. Higgs (1895).

36. C. Hull (1895).

37. E. Fitzmaurice (1895).

38. J. Aubrey (1813).

39. H. Higgs (1895a).

40. C. Hull (1900).

41. M. Pasquier (1903).

42. S. Matsukawa (1955) and subsequently P.D. Groenewegen (1967).

43. W. Muller (1932).

44. E.A.G. Johnson (1937).

45. E. Strauss (1954).

46. W. Letwin (1956).

47. W. Letwin (1963).

48. M. Bowley (1973).

49. S. Matsukawa (1965).

50. L. Einaudi (1941, pp. 372–76).

51. G. Pietranera (1963, pp. 31–50).

52. U. Cerroni (1973).

53. P. Bora (1980).

54. M. Holtrop (1928, 1929).
55. R.T. Selden (1956).

Chapter 2

1. The various assessments are reported in J. Schumpeter (1967, pp. 209ff.) and E. Cannan (1964, pp. 14–17). Hicks (1983, p. 17–18) takes a different view, considering Petty as the "Father of Social Accounting," noting his influence on Cantillon and Quesnay's *Tableau Economique*.

2. Even Adam Smith interprets Petty in this sense when he says: "I have no great faith in political arithmetick" (1976, p. 534). Smith's observation is interesting because it highlights, with respect to what will be suggested later in this section, the extent to which he departs from the quantitative approach followed by Petty, instead favoring the qualitative description of economic phenomena.

3. K. Marx (1971, p. 53). Cf. also F. Engels (1962, p. 317) where Petty is called the "founder of modern political economy." Engels tells us (Ibid., p. 14) that the passages concerning Petty (pp. 317–20) were written by Marx himself. According to G. Pietranera (1963, pp. 46–47), Marx distinguished "Petty, the economist," who "gave birth to the entire theory of value in exchange (and, naturally, of labor, its division, and of capital)," from "Petty, the political arithmetist," who "was responsible for research into the nominal values of things"; Marx considered political arithmetic as "nothing more than 'the first form in which political economy is treated as a separate science.' " K. Marx, (Ibid., pp. 53–54). But the "nothing more than" represents Pietranera's judgment, not Marx's so that at least in this respect his view of Marx's interpretation of Petty's work must be considered as questionable.

4. Cf. C. Hull (1963, pp. 239–40).

5. W. Petty (1927a, p. 15), letter to Southwell dated 3 November 1687.

6. See the very first sentence of the Preface to *The Political Anatomy of Ireland* (1963, p. 129). (The passage is quoted above, p. 24.) Acceptance of Bacon's methodology is also apparent in the activity of the Royal Society, of which Petty was a founder and very active member (cf. above, section 1.4), and in the project for a *History of Trades* set out in Petty (1648) with explicit reference to Bacon, and repeated in a note published in Petty (1927, pp. 205–7).

7. F. Bacon, *Novum Organum*, Book I of the Aphorisms, No. 95.

8. Petty (1963, p. 244). In a recently published *Dialogue*, Petty asks "Can you apply Arithmetick to Every Thing?" and replies in the affirmative: "Unless They bee Mysticall Spirituall eternell &c." See Matsukawa (1977, p. 48).

9. G. Galilei (1890–1909, p. 232), *Il Saggiatore*.

10. In this regard Petty's position concerning *transplantation*, discussed in section 1.2 above, should be kept in mind, as well as what will be seen later in this chapter concerning the "law of nature," and what will be said in the discussion of the rate of interest and the rejection of the Scholastic condemnation of usury in section 3.5.

11. In this respect Bacon's reference to Machiavelli is instructive: "We are much beholden to Machiavel and others, that write what men do, and not what they ought to do" (Bacon, 1965, p. 165). Obviously science, i.e., the study of "what men do" can, indeed should, then be utilized as a guide for behavior and practical intervention; this is the meaning of Petty's statement: "I meane by Politiques . . . the way how to keep a people in Peace & plenty" (Matsukawa, 1977, p. 37).

12. The debates on international trade in the seventeenth century were strongly influenced by the relationship of the various authors to the East India Company; theoretical arguments were adapted to attack or defend the interests of the Company according to the author's financial interests. This relationship was particularly close in

the case of authors such as Thomas Mun (*Discourse on Trade*, 1621) and Josiah Child (*Observations on Commerce*, 1668).

13. Petty (1963, p. 129).

14. For example, in the passage from *The Political Anatomy of Ireland* quoted in the next section, Petty explicitly declares that knowledge of the "body politick" is a precondition for operating on it.

15. "The economists have a singular manner of proceeding. There are for them only two kinds of institutions: those of art and those of nature. Feudal institutions are artificial institutions, those of the bourgeoisie are natural institutions. In this they resemble the theologians, who also establish two kinds of religion. Every religion but their own is an invention of man, while their own religion is an emanation from God. In saying that existing conditions—the conditions of bourgeois production—are natural, the economists give it to be understood that these are the relations in which wealth is created and the productive forces are developed conformably to the laws of nature. Thus these relations are themselves natural laws, independent of the influence of time. They are eternal laws which must always govern society. Thus there has been history, but there is no longer any." K. Marx (no date, p. 131). Cf. also, Marx (1970, p. 81, n. 2).

16. We will return to the question of the importance of this comparison for economic theory in chapter 6. Here we shall only point out that it has a long tradition which can be traced back to the celebrated apology of Menenio Agrippa. The age-old formulation takes on a new significance, however, with the discovery of the circulation of blood by Harvey and the introduction of the new philosophical approach to science in which the State—Hobbes' *Leviathan*—is considered as an "artificial man" who, like man himself, is conceived of as a machine (cf. T. Hobbes, 1946, pp. 5–6). It is for this reason that the new logic of quantities (arithmetic and geometry) developed in the natural sciences was appropriate to the study of the "body politick."

17. Petty (1963, p. 9). According to Hull (1963, p. 9, n. 1), the phrase "*Res nolunt male administrari*" was a favorite of Petty's and its authorship was attributed to him by his contemporaries, but it is to be found in Aristotle's *Metaphysica*.

18. Ibid., p. 60. Hull (1963, p. 60, n. 1) attributes the Latin quote to Horace's *Epistolae*.

19. *Petty* (1963, p. 9). And in his *Political Arithmetick* he complains that "too many Matters have been regulated by Laws, which Nature, long Custom, and general Consent, ought only to have governed" (1963, p. 243). As A.W. Coats (1975) points out, even Adam Smith "did not use the term 'natural' as equivalent to 'inevitable' . . . but, in accordance with contemporary usage, . . . as equivalent to 'normal'— . . . what normally occurs or would occur in the absence of some human, legal or institutional impediment. . . . However," Coats also notes, "the term 'natural' was also used to connote 'ideal,' and . . . there is an important tension between the 'natural' and 'moral' elements in Smith's work."

This element of contradiction inherent in Smith's work can already be seen in the difference between Quesnay's economic research and the conception set out in his *Droit Naturel*, cf. Quesnay (1765 and 1958). On Quesnay see Ridolfi (1973).

20. See above, section 1.3 in relation to the land registry, and below, sections 4.2 and 4.3 on customs duties, section 3.3 on banks, and section 7.4 on wages.

21. K. Marx (1970, p. 9), Preface to the first edition. Cf. note 15 above.

22. "Omnia in mensura et numero et pondere disposuisti" (*Bible*, Sap. 11: 21). Petty also derives from the Bible the motto for his *Discourse of Duplicate Proportion* (Petty, 1963, p. 638): "Pondere, Mensura et Numero Deus omnia fecit: Mensuram et Pondus Numero, Numero omnia fecit." The idea that the pure numerical proportions among elements constitute the essence of the universe in the act of its creation is also maintained in Plato's *Timeo*, and represents a focal point of the neo-Platonic tradition.

23. S. Pufendorf (1934, p. 731). It should be recalled that Pufendorf was a representative of the natural law doctrine which Petty implicitly opposes in his works.

24. See, for example, Petty's letter to J. Aubrey dated 29 May 1678 quoted by E. Fitzmaurice (1895, p. 258).

25. Petty (1963, pp. 129–30). This passage reflects an *a priori* optimism concerning the method of the "new science" which was widely held at the time. Any inadequacy in the results achieved by the analysis was not attributed to the method itself, but to the instruments available to apply it. These were considered as capable of further perfection. It also demonstrates how the analysis was considered as the process of dissection into elementary parts and their recomposition as a synthesis.

26. For Ricardo's explicit statements on the issue cf. Ricardo (1951b, p. 318) and (1952a, p. 337). In fact Ricardo, who does not refer directly to Petty's work in his own writing, adopts the same methodological characteristics discussed in this chapter in their purest form in his analysis, from the choice of quantifiable phenomena as the objects of analysis to the method of abstraction. An essential link in the chain that leads from Petty to Quesnay to Ricardo is represented by the work of R. Cantillon, *Essai sur la Nature du Commerce en Général* (cf. also Hicks, 1983. The *Essai* was published posthumously in 1775, some twenty years after the author's death). In addition to using Petty's work as a point of departure for his analysis of the problem of value (as we shall see in chapter 7), Cantillon adopts his methodology, adding a number of improvements which would prove fundamental to Ricardian analysis (cf. R. Cantillon, 1931). "One of the practices which Cantillon applies consistently is the isolating of the factors under investigation in order to consider their effects in a hypothetical situation which is not perturbed by extraneous influences. This was important because it went beyond the method of successive approximation, resolving a problem by first setting it out in its simplest form, developing it by means of a series of intermediate specifications" (P. Capitani, 1975, p. 26).

27. Petty (1963, p. 129). Political arithmetic is thus presented as the instrument of analysis especially adapted to the new medical-political science of the body-machine (cf. note 16 above).

Chapter 3

1. Liberal historians of economic thought, from Adam Smith onward, go so far as to attribute to Petty's contemporaries, classified as "mercantilists," the view that precious metals are identical to wealth. Some, such as L. Einaudi (1932, p. 219–25) locate the birth of economic science in the rejection of this identity (e.g., Botero—Petty—Cantillon). For a criticism of this view see J. Schumpeter (1967, pp. 360–62). Petty explicitly rejects the identity of wealth and precious metals in his *Quantulumcumque Concerning Money* (1963, p. 446). See also the passage quoted in note 2.

2. The comparison, used for example by Hobbes (1974, pp. 22–24), between money and blood owed its popularity to the contemporary discovery of the circulation of blood by William Harvey. For Petty "the blood and nutritive juyces of the Body Politick" are the "product of Husbandry and Manufacture" (*A Treatise of Taxes and Contributions*, 1963, p. 28).

3. *Verbum Sapienti* in Petty (1963, p. 112). Petty gives another interesting definition of money in a brief glossary of economic terms: "Money. Is the common measure of commodityes. A common bond of every man upon every man. The equivalent of commodityes" (1927, p. 210).

4. For example, in the quotation of the preceding note; in *A Treatise of Taxes and Contributions* (1963, pp. 44ff.); or in *The Political Anatomy of Ireland* (1963, pp. 183–84).

5. See chapter 6, section 6. The consideration of money as a "store of value" (Keynes) is not the same thing as considering it the "material representative and general form of wealth," (Marx) but the first aspect might be considered a phenomenon explained by the second, and thus implicitly contained in it. Petty hints at the social function of money in the passage quoted in note 3.

6. *Political Anatomy of Ireland* (1963, p. 183).

7. Cf. for example, Petty (1927a, pp. 231–32), *A Treatise of Taxes and Contributions* (1963, p. 44) where Petty, starting from the variability of money, concludes by considering land and labor as "natural" measures of value (this question will be further discussed in chapter 8, below), and *Quantulumcumque Concerning Money* (1963, pp. 437ff).

8. For the discussions surrounding metallic v. fiduciary, and bimetallic standards see J. Schumpeter (1967, pp. 288ff.).

9. *A Dialogue on Political Arithmetick* (reprinted in Matsukawa, 1977, p. 47).

10. *Verbum Sapienti* (1963, p. 113).

11. *Quantulumcumque Concerning Money* (1963, p. 441).

12. Ibid., The depreciation of money will be discussed more fully in chapter 4, section 4 with respect to the consequences for foreign trade.

13. See the passages quoted in notes 6 and 7. Petty, true to his times, preferred silver to gold.

14. "So as it becomes a Trade to study and make Advantages of these Irregularities, to the prejudice of the good People, who are taught, that whatever is called Money, is the same, and regular, and uniform, and a just Measure of all Commodities. For whence it hath happened, that all English Money which hath a great and deserved Reputation in the World for its intrinsick Goodness, is quite carried away out of Ireland, and such Money brought instead of it, as these studied Merchants do from time to time bring in for their Advantage upon the Common People, their Credulity and Ignorance" *Political Anatomy of Ireland* (1963, p. 184). This passage enunciates what has come to be known as "Gresham's Law," which had already been formulated by several authors in the sixteenth and seventeenth centuries.

15. Cf. for example, *A Treatise of Taxes and Contributions* (1963, pp. 35–37); *Verbum Sapienti* (1963, p. 112).

16. Petty emphasizes repeatedly that money is but a part (and a relatively small one) of national wealth. In *Verbum Sapienti* (1963, pp. 114, 117) he estimates the share of money in national wealth at 6/667 and 11/50 in national income. In *The Political Anatomy of Ireland* (1963, p. 193) he evaluates the share of money to national expenditure in Ireland at 1/10.

17. This logical consequence of his conception of money is not made explicit by Petty himself, who limits his comments to recalling that an excess of money is possible, but that it would not create great difficulty (because such excess "May be soon turn'd into the magnificence of Gold and Silver Vessels") unless the policies adopted in order to carry useless money to the country were to lead to a destruction of national wealth. Cf. *The Political Anatomy of Ireland* (1963, p. 193) and also *A Treatise of Taxes and Contributions* (1963, pp. 36–37).

The "service as an instrument of production" played by precious metals when "they replace labour" is clearly explained by Marx: "Without money, a mass of swaps would be necessary before one obtained the desired article in exchange. Furthermore, in each particular exchange one would have to undertake an investigation into the relative value of commodities. Money spares us the first task in its role as instrument of exchange (instrument of commerce); the second task, as measure of value and representative of all commodities. . . . The opposite assertion, that money is *not* productive, amounts only to saying that, apart from fluctuations in which it is productive, as measure, instrument of circulation, and representative of value, it is *unproductive*; that its quantity is productive only in so far as it is necessary to fulfill these preconditions. That it becomes not only *unproductive*, but *faux frais de production*, the moment when more of it is employed than necessary for its productive aspect—this is a truth that holds for every other instrument of production or exchange; for the machine as well as the means of transportation" (1973, pp. 215–16).

18. The creation of a land bank is proposed in Petty (1963, pp. 26, 35–36, 265–66, 311–12, 573) and (1972, pp. 31, 78, 87, 270–71) as well as in numerous other places. On the proposed land register, considered a prerequisite for the operation of the land bank, see chapter 6, note 10. Proposals similar to Petty's were common at that time. Before John Law, at the beginning of the eighteenth century, the best known supporter of the land bank (in practice as well as theory) was probably Nicholas Barbon (*Discourse of Trade*, 1690), although the proposal of William Potter (*The Key of Wealth*, 1650) was even earlier. Adam Smith also adopted a position similar to Petty's: "The substitution of paper in the room of gold and silver money, replaces a very expensive instrument of commerce with one much less costly, and sometimes equally convenient. Circulation comes to be carried out by a new wheel, which it costs less both to erect and to maintain than the old one" (1976, p. 292).

19. *Verbum Sapienti* (1963, pp. 112–13). See also *A Treatise of Taxes and Contributions* (1963, pp. 35–36), *The Political Anatomy of Ireland* (1963, p. 187); *Quantulumcumque Concerning Money* (1963, p. 446) and *Political Arithmetick* (1963, pp. 310–11).

20. J. Locke (1691), R. Cantillon (1931), as well as Holtrop (1928, 1929). Professor Groenewegen has pointed out to me that Petty's analysis of the velocity of circulation of money is referred to and employed by Marshall in *Money, Credit and Commerce* (1923, p. 47).

21. See, for example, *A Treatise of Taxes and Contributions* (1963, pp. 36–37).

22. Ibid., p. 57. See also *Quantulumcumque Concerning Money* (1963, p. 445). The embargo on the export of precious metals was abolished in England in 1663. An interesting debate, involving authors such as Malynes, Misselden, and Mun, which represented a significant advance in the theory of international trade, developed concerning the embargo, and the exceptions to it that were accorded to the large trading companies such as the East India Company.

23. See, for example, *Verbum Sapienti* (1963, p. 119).

24. *Political Arithmetick* (1963, p. 313).

25. *A Treatise of Taxes and Contributions* (1963, p. 60).

26. *Political Arithmetick* (1963, p. 269).

27. K. Marx (1973, p. 232). The absence of historical perspective, however, prevented Petty from recognizing the connection between the development of production for the market and money taking on the characteristic of the representative and general form of wealth.

28. Ibid., pp. 228 ff.

29. *Quantulumcumque Concerning Money* (1963, p. 446).

30. Ibid., See also *A Treatise of Taxes and Contributions* (1963, p. 47) and (1927, p. 211).

31. J. Schumpeter (1967) refers to the point several times, see also R. Tawney (1975).

32. *A Treatise of Taxes and Contributions* (1963, p. 48); see also *Quantulumcumque Concerning Money* (1963, pp. 447–48) and (1927, p. 246). J. Locke (1691) follows Petty on this point, as on a number of other monetary questions. On the basis of statements such as this E. Böhm-Bawerk (1932, pp. 61–69) interpreted Petty's (and others, in particular, Turgot's) theory of interest as a "fructification theory," implying that these authors considered money capable of the *creation* of a net product. Schumpeter (1967, p. 332 n.) criticizes Böhm-Bawerk's interpretation, add-

ing that Petty's statements should be considered as equilibrium propositions, while as a theory of interest they suffer from circularity "because the value of land itself depends upon the rate of interest." It is not possible to identify a causal relation: Is the rate of interest 10% because land with a value of 1000 earns an annual rental of 100 or is the value of the land 1000 because its rental is 100 and the rate of interest is 10%? The relation between real phenomena and monetary phenomena is simply affirmed, not explained. However, it should not be forgotten that Petty determined the value of land independently of the rate of interest on the basis of rent and social-institutional elements (cf. *A Treatise of Taxes and Contributions* [1963, p. 45]) thereby avoiding the circular reasoning criticized by Schumpeter. The argument, in particular as it applies to Turgot, is discussed in Groenewegen (1971).

33. *A Treatise of Taxes and Contributions* (1963, p. 48), see also *Quantulumcumque Concerning Money* (1963, pp. 252) and (1927, p. 246).

34. *A Treatise of Taxes and Contributions* (1963, p. 48), see also *Quantulumcumque Concerning Money* (1963, pp. 447–48) and (1927, p. 247). The history of the controversy surrounding the legislation of a maximum rate of interest is given in G. Tucker (1960, pp. 7–29).

35. The discussion of the rate of interest confirms the interpretation of the concept of "natural law" discussed in chapter 2, section 2. While Aristotle, the scholastics, and other supporters of natural law (who referred to "natural law" to condemn the payment of interest) considered "natural" as being "just," i.e., consistent with the law of the Divine, Petty thought of "natural law" as nothing more than the result of the operation of the forces intrinsic to the functioning of the system. Only by taking certain passages in which Petty justifies interest as "A Reward for forbearing the use of your own Money" out of context would it be possible to equate Petty's position with the "moral" judgment adopted by the authors of the natural law tradition. In fact, there can be no doubt that at the same time Petty argues against the moral condemnation of interest within the conceptual apparatus of his antagonists, he proposes a radical change of view that transforms the concepts used, such as natural law, and the very problem under discussion, shifting it from the moral judgment of the phenomenon of interest to the logical explanation of its existence and manifestation (that is, its level).

36. *The Political Anatomy of Ireland* (1963, p. 187), *Report From the Council of Trade* (1963, pp. 221–22), and (1927, p. 247).

37. The low rate of interest in Holland is referred to as an example of its superiority relative to other countries: "As for lowness of Interest [in Holland], it is also a necessary effect of all premisses, and not the Fruit of their contrivance," *Political Arithmetick* (1963, p. 261). A few pages earlier Petty specifies that "The natural fall of Interest, is the effect of the increase of Money" (Ibid., p. 304). The question is also referred to in (*Ibid.*, pp. 243, 254), (1927, p. 247) and (1927a, p. 185).

38. In relation to the land registry and the banks see the reference in chapter 1, note 10 and chapter 6, note 10 as well as note 17 of this chapter. Petty (1927, p. 246) asserts the position emphatically: "Where banks are interest will be low."

Chapter 4

1. See, for example, J. Viner (1964, pp. 15–22).
2. See chapter 6, section 5.
3. See chapter 6, section 6.
4. *Political Arithmetick* (1963, p. 259).
5. Ibid., p. 260, see also (1927a, p. 236). The argument is discussed in chapter 7, section 3. The reader should note that Petty did not himself employ the modern

terminology used in the text.

6. *Political Arithmetick* (1963, p. 259).

7. See chapter 3, section 4. For a pointed rejection of sectoral controls (that liberal historians would identify as "bullionist" prescriptions) in favor of the less restrictive point of view covering the balance of payments as a whole, cf. *Quantulumcumque Concerning Money* (1963, p. 441). See also (1927, p. 189): "That England is one party, and all the rest of the world the other." For the distinction between bullionist and mercantilist cf. J. Viner (1964, pp. 3–5), and for a criticism of this distinction, J. Schumpeter (1967, pp. 336ff.).

8. *Verbum Sapienti* (1963, p. 119), *Political Arithmetick* (1963, pp. 271, 309).

9. Note that Petty distinguishes capital movements from the movement of goods (*Political Arithmetick*, 1963, p. 313) so that even if current terminology is not employed, the balance of payments is distinguished from the trade balance. On this point see J. Viner (1964, pp. 13–15). On the utility of encouraging immigration of skilled labor, see, for example, *A Treatise of Taxes and Contributions* (1963, pp. 59–60).

10. See, for example, *Political Arithmetick* (1963, pp. 257–58), and (1927, pp. 209–10), (1927a, p. 236). By "world market" Petty obviously means only the most developed countries linked by a network of trade relations, i.e., about 80 million people in a world population of some 300 million according to the estimates of *Political Arithmetick* (1963, p. 295).

11. Cf., for example, *The Political Anatomy of Ireland* (1963, p. 187).

12. Cf., for example, *Verbum Sapienti* (1963, pp. 118–19).

13. *A Treatise of Taxes and Contributions* (1963, pp. 55–56).

14. Cf. *A Treatise of Taxes and Contributions* (1963, p. 91).

15. *Political Arithmetick* (1963, p. 271); Petty points out the obvious fact that duties may also serve as a reprisal against other countries who have adopted protectionist policies.

16. (1927, pp. 89–90).

17. *Report From the Council of Trade* (1963, p. 222). The demonstration effect is presented in J. Duesenberry (1969, chapter 3, p. 31).

18. *A Treatise of Taxes and Contributions* (1963, p. 56).

19. On Colbert's policy see, for example, F. Carsten (1969, pp. 38–46).

20. *A Treatise of Taxes and Contributions* (1963, pp. 58–60).

21. Cf. *The Political Anatomy of Ireland* (1963, p. 160), *Political Arithmetick* (1963, pp. 298–99).

22. Cf. *Political Arithmetick* (1963, p. 298). The various proposals for *transplantation*, or the mass deportation of the Irish in England should be recalled (cf. chapter 6, section 7).

23. "To remit so many great Sums out of Ireland into England, when all Trade between the two said Kingdoms is prohibited, must be very chargeable; for now the Goods which go out of Ireland, in order to furnish the said sums in England, must for England go into the Barbados, and there be sold for Sugars, which brought into England, are sold for Money to pay there what Ireland owes. Which way being so long, tedious and hazardous, must necessarily so raise the exchange of money, as we have seen 15 per Cent. frequently given. . . ." *The Political Anatomy of Ireland* (1963, p. 185).

24. *A Treatise of Taxes and Contributions* (1963, p. 46), see also *The Political Anatomy of Ireland* (1963, pp. 185, 197) and *Report from the Council of Trade* (1963, p. 216). Petty's observation is adopted and expanded by Josiah Child in his *Discourse about Trade* (1690).

25. For the history of the debate on this question see, for example, J. Viner (1964, pp. 74ff.).

26. Petty defines exchange as "Local Interest, or a Reward given for having your

Money at such a Place where you most need the use of it'' *Quantulumcumque Concerning Money* (1963, p. 447).

27. *The Political Anatomy of Ireland* (1963, p. 185).

28. *A Treatise of Taxes and Contributions* (1963, pp. 87–88).

29. Some commentators have praised Petty for adopting a less rigid protectionist position than his contemporaries. However, these are "political" evaluations which are quite irrelevant from our point of view. In any case, to give just one example, the writings of North must be assigned more importance in this respect.

Chapter 5

1. M. Pasquier (1903, p. 243).

2. *Political Arithmetick* (1963, p. 298). On the relation between positive and natural laws see chapter 2, section 2. Petty's position on the problem of taxation confirms the interpretation given there.

3. Ibid. p. 302. In reality, the same initial system of taxation, appropriate for a feudal economy, cannot be considered adequate for a society that is moving towards the industrial revolution. Petty does not, as we have pointed out in section 2.2, recognize the historically determined character of "laws of nature."

4. Ibid. p. 301. In this case Petty's theoretical view corresponds directly to his private interests as a landowner in conflict with the *farmers of publick revenue*.

5. Cf. *A Treatise of Taxes and Contributions*, chapter XI (1963, pp. 74–77). The passage cited is on p. 76.

6. *A Treatise of Taxes and Contributions* (1963, p. 21).

7. Ibid., p. 32. See also, p. 26.

8. *The Political Anatomy of Ireland* (1963, pp. 193–94).

9. *Political Arithmetick* (1963, p. 244). See also the discussion of the problem in chapter 7, section 4.

10. Petty considered a tax of 10% on wages to be feasible, and that workers would prefer to pay it, working 1/20th more and consuming 1/20th less, rather than resorting to an armed uprising. *Verbum Sapienti* (1963, pp. 110); see also *Political Arithmetick* (1963, pp. 305–6). On the other hand, as we shall see in chapter 7, section 4, Petty believed that wages in excess of the subsistence minimum were conducive to indolence, cf. *Political Arithmetick* (1963, pp. 274–75) and *A Treatise of Taxes and Contributions* (1963, pp. 137–38) where Petty seems to exclude workers from the "public" whose well-being concerns him.

11. *A Treatise of Taxes and Contributions*, chapter XV: "Of Excize" (1963, p. 91).

12. Ibid. p. 95. Petty refers to a scheme of taxation of consumption in which the tax was higher the more useless the consumption expenditure that had been adopted with good effect in Holland. *Political Arithmetick* (1963, p. 271). The idea of a proportional tax on consumption expenditures has its origins in the writings of the natural law philosophers (Hobbes). More recently the attractiveness of a tax related to expenditures rather than income has been supported by L. Einaudi ("Intorno al concetto di reddito imponibile e di un sistema di imposta sul reddito consumato," 1912, and "Contributo alla ricerca dell'ottima imposte," 1923, both reprinted in Einaudi, 1941, which also contains an essay on "L'imposta in Hobbes, Petty e Bosellini") and, for rather different reasons, by N. Kaldor (1955).

13. *A Treatise of Taxes and Contributions*, chapters II and III (1963, pp. 21–37).

14. In chapter VII of *Political Arithmetick* (1963, pp. 305–6) Petty suggests that tax receipts of a tenth of total private expenditures would be sufficient to cover government expenditure needs; and observes that, in the presence of positive private saving, taxes would represent less than 10% of national income.

15. Ibid., p. 271.

16. Ibid., p. 295.

17. *A Treatise of Taxes and Contributions* (1963, p. 32).

18. Ibid., p. 34.

19. Ibid., pp. 35–36.

20. Cf., for example, Petty (1927, pp. 88, 95–96).

21. *A Treatise of Taxes and Contributions* (1963, pp. 91–92).

22. Cf., for example, *A Treatise of Taxes and Contributions*, chapter X (1963, pp. 67–73). The fines should be set so as to make crime unprofitable, taking account of the probability that the perpetrator of the crime is apprehended and brought to justice. Thus, in the case of theft, the fine should be equal to 2n times the value of the theft if the thief is apprehended in 1/n of the cases reported. Ibid., p. 69.

23. Ibid., p. 54.

24. Ibid., p. 55. See the discussion of customs duties and international trade in chapter 4.

25. Ibid., Cf. above, note 22.

26. Cf., for example, *The Political Anatomy of Ireland* (1963, pp. 160–61).

27. *A Treatise of Taxes and Contributions* (1963, p. 84).

28. See, for example, M. Ashley (1970, pp. 121–80) particularly, p. 124.

29. *Political Arithmetic*, chapter II, entitled "That Some Kind of Taxes and Publick Levies, May Rather Increase than Diminish the Wealth of the Kingdom" (1963, pp. 268–69). See also *A Treatise of Taxes and Contributions* (1963, pp. 30, 32–33, 37).

30. *Political Arithmetick* (1963, pp. 269–70). These statements are linked to the criterion (durability of the product) used by Petty to establish a ranking of the various sectors in terms of their importance for the national wealth (cf. chapter 6, section 6).

31. The reader is referred to the discussion of the functions of the State in the following chapter. Petty groups public expenditures in six categories: 1. military expenditures, which in normal times would alone represent one-half of the total; 2. expenditures to maintain the Court, and the administrative and judicial systems; 3. religious expenditures, considered necessary for the maintenance of order and justice; 4. educational expenditures, which could not be left to private initiative because impartial selection could not be guaranteed; 5. social expenditures made necessary, among other things, by the policy of wage controls supported by Petty himself ("it is unjust to let any starve, when we think it just to limit the wages of the poor, so as they can lay up nothing against the time of their impotency and want of work"); 6. infrastructure, such as roads, bridges, navigable rivers, aqueducts, ports, and so forth. *A Treatise of Taxes and Contributions*, chapter I (1963, pp. 18–20).

32. Ibid., chapter II, pp. 21–31. Petty criticizes in particular the excessive number of priests, lawyers, judges, students, and university teachers.

33. Public works policies are frequently proposed by Petty, cf., for example, *Political Arithmetick* (1963, pp. 269, 307), *The Political Anatomy of Ireland* (1963, pp. 147, 217–18).

34. *A Treatise of Taxes and Contributions* (1963, p. 31).

35. *Political Arithmetick* (1963, p. 317). Petty used the calculations to show "that there are spare Hands enough among the King of England's subjects, to earn two Millions per annum more than they now do; and that there are also Employments, ready, proper, and sufficient, for that purpose" (Ibid.). See also Petty (1927, p. 194): "By knowing the number of working hands of between 10 and 70, and the number of these already employed in Trade & faculties of gaine, it may bee knowne how many spare hands there are, & consequently what new trades may be introduced without destroying what are already."

36. Building on Keynes definition (cf. J.M. Keynes, 1936, p. 289), the concept of

potential full-employment income has recently been proposed as an empirical concept by A.M. Okun (1962).

Chapter 6

1. See, for example, Petty's writings on the prerogatives of the King, the various legislative organs and the government in (1927, pp. 5–21). On Petty's political conception in relation to the political transformations that were then occurring in Europe, see M. Pasquier (1903, pp. 43ff.).

2. K. Marx (1973, p. 108). It should be noted that in *A Dialogue on Political Arithmetick* (reprinted in Matsukawa, 1977, pp. 45–46) Petty defines "The Naturall & Intrinsic strength of any Country" as based on the difference between the total working population and the "Necessary labour," i.e., the number of laborers necessary to produce food for the whole population. These are concepts strikingly similar to the Marxian notions of "necessary" and "surplus" labor. The analogy is strengthened by Petty's noting "that all the people working None need worke full 2 dayes in the week" (Ibid., p. 50), thus indicating the magnitude of the existing surplus labor.

3. Even though Machiavelli's works appeared on the Index and as such were forbidden, they were widely read throughout Europe. Petty could have read them, from the time he was a boy attending the Jesuit school in Caen (in the most sophisticated of the religious orders the reading of works on the Index was a normal occurrence), or in Paris where he studied with Hobbes whose works, as is well known, were strongly influenced by Machiavelli's ideas, or in England after his return in 1644 (the works of the Florentine writer were widely diffused in the country: *Art of War* was translated in 1563, *History of Florence* in 1595, *Discourses* in 1636, and *The Prince* in 1640). In any event Petty was also able to read both Latin and French, languages in which numerous editions of these works appeared.

4. In terms of their conceptions of the State, Sraffa proposed a link between Machiavelli and Petty to Gramsci in whose *Prison Notebooks* the theme reappeared. Cf. A. Gramsci (1968, p. 589) letter of March 14, 1932, and April 27, 1932 (1968, p. 616, from Tatiana Schucht to Gramsci) and (1975, pp. 1038–39): "If one shows that Machiavelli sought to establish links between city and the countryside and to enlarge the function of the city dwellers to the point of requiring them to give up certain feudal-corporative privileges with respect to the countryside, in order to incorporate the country dwellers into the State, then one also demonstrates that Machiavelli's thought had implicitly overcome the mercantilist phase and already shows signs of a physiocratic character, that is, he is thinking of a political-social context which is that presumed by classical economics. Professor Sraffa calls attention to a possible similarity of Machiavelli to an English economist of the seventeenth century, William Petty, that Marx calls the 'founder of classical economics.' "

5. On this point, cf. Gramsci (1975, pp. 1276–77, 1350, 1477–78).

6. A. Gramsci (1971, p. 143). "[C]ity and countryside" correspond to manufacturing and agriculture, the two sectors in which modern productive activity was initially divided.

7. In this sense it is possible to give more precision to Gramsci's (1975, p. 692) definition: "economic life is a continous fabric of exchanges of property": The economic system is the framework in which economic life thus understood takes place, being made up of a series of sectors which reciprocally guarantee the means of production necessary to each, by means of a continuous fabric of *necessary* exchanges of property.

8. Cf. F. Quesnay (1958).

9. Cf. chapter 1, section 3.

10. Cf. chapter 1, section 3, especially note 10. Petty emphasizes that "there can be no incouragement to Industry, where there is no assurance of what shall be gotten by it" (*Political Arithmetick*, 1963, p. 264), observes that the greater security of property would increase the value of land, (*A Treatise of Taxes and Contributions*, 1963, p. 46), and recalls that the creation of a land register would make the collection of taxes easier (1927, pp. 88, 95–96), reduce the work required of lawyers (1963, pp. 26, 264–65) and the amount of money needed for circulation (1963, pp. 66, 573; 1927a, p. 257) thereby freeing labor and resources for use in directly productive activities. Petty attaches a great deal of importance to his proposal, so much so as to include the land registry among the "Ten Tooles for Making the Crowne and State of England more powerful than any other now in Europe" (1927, p. 256).

11. In this regard Gramsci's (1975, p. 1350) observation seems appropriate: "there was a period in which 'science' could not exist, not only because there were no scientists, but because the preconditions which create those particular 'regularities' or 'automatisms' whose study provides the origin of scientific research were not present."

12. See above, section 6.5.

13. F. Quesnay (1958, p. 758).

14. Although A. Smith (1976) explicitly rejects the physiocratic position which considers agriculture as the only productive sector (pp. 663–78) he nonetheless places agriculture at the top of the ranking that he makes of the different sectors in order of their productivity because it produces "two surpluses" (pp. 330, 675).

15. "But the labour of the manufacturer fixes and realizes itself in some particular subject or vendible commodity, which lasts for some time at least after that labour is past. . . . The labour of the menial servant, on the contrary, does not fix or realize itself in any particular subject or vendible commodity" (A. Smith, 1976, p. 330).

16. K. Marx (1969, pp. 152ff.).

17. Cf. A. Smith (1976, p. 333).

18. W. Petty (1963, p. 270), italics added. See also (1927, p. 213).

19. Surplus labor could also be found in commerce, for example, in the excessive number of brewers in Ireland, see Petty (1963, p. 146).

20. See, for example, Petty (1963, pp. 23–29, 146). Petty takes the trouble to indicate the methods that could be used to estimate the strictly necessary number of soldiers, priests, and doctors, cf. (1927, pp. 195–97).

21. See, in particular, Petty (1963, pp. 26, 28).

22. Petty (1963, p. 256, as well as pp. 289–90).

23. Ibid., p. 269, as well as Petty (1927, p. 211).

24. In contrast to Petty, Smith (1976, pp. 346–49) does not consider labor that produces goods that are more durable as more productive; but rather, more correctly, considers expenditure on more durable goods as more favorable to accumulation and thus to the expansion of productive labor: houses are better than dogs or horses or food. K. Marx (1969, p. 174) ignores this difference when he observes that in this respect "Adam Smith also falls back more or less into the Mercantilist conception of 'permanency,' " and refers in particular to Petty.

25. Petty (1963, p. 269). Nearly the same words are used some pages earlier (Ibid., pp. 259–60) and would be used again (1927, pp. 213–14).

26. See, for example, Petty (1963, p. 259).

27. Cf., for example, Ibid., p. 267.

28. It is in this sense that it might be possible to interpret a hint on this problem contained in one of Petty's youthful works which is more radical than the position adopted in his more strictly economic works: "We see that all Countries where Manufactures and Trades flourish, as Holland, etc., become potent and rich." In fact, the young Petty explains, unproductive laborers would naturally diminish because each

would be able to choose to undertake productive labor which would allow him to live "in more plenty and honour" (1648, pp. 22–23).

29. *A Treatise of Taxes and Contributions*, chapter II (1963, p. 22).

30. Petty (1927, p. 78).

31. *The Political Anatomy of Ireland* (1963, p. 223).

32. The different estimates that Petty gives for the value of a person should not be a cause of surprise for they depend on a number of different circumstances, including those that influence the productivity of labor. The value of a person is estimated, for example, at 69 pounds sterling in *Verbum Sapienti* (1963, p. 108) and 70 pounds in *The Political Anatomy of Ireland* (1963, p. 152), *A Treatise of Ireland* (1963, p. 563), *Another Essay in Political Arithmetick* (1963, p. 476), and in Petty (1927a, pp. 55–6, 232). The figure is more than 80 pounds in *Political Arithmetick* (1963, p. 267) and *A Treatise of Ireland* (1963, p. 600). Finally, Petty believes that he can evaluate "the people who have been destroyed in Ireland during the rebellion, as Slaves and Negroes are usually rated, viz. at about 15£. one with another," *The Political Anatomy of Ireland* (1963, p. 152).

33. See, for example, *Verbum Sapienti* (1963, p. 117).

34. *A Treatise of Taxes and Contributions* (1963, p. 34). See also *Political Arithmetick* (1963, pp. 255, 300).

35. See, for example, *Political Arithmetick* (1963, p. 286).

36. Thus, in a list of the duties of the Sovereign, Petty places the increase of the population directly after peace and freedom of religion (Petty, 1927, p. 7).

37. Cf., for example, Petty (1963, pp. 157–58), (1927, p. 267), and (1927a, pp. 47–58). In the latter, various writings are reprinted in a section called "Multiplication of Mankind" (one of these, entitled *Californian Marriages* proposes a strange form of eugenic commune; various laws are also proposed which virtually require men and women to engage in forced procreation). Lansdowne calls an increase in population "Petty's favourite panacea" (Petty, 1927a, p. 126).

38. This proposal called for the transfer of virtually the entire Irish population to England where it would increase the density of the population and thus increase the productivity of labor and the level of wealth. Ireland, on the other hand, was to be transformed into an immense cattle farm in which only 300,000 persons would remain. Cf., for example, *A Treatise of Ireland* (1963, pp. 551ff.), *The Political Anatomy of Ireland* (1963, pp. 157–58), and Petty (1927, p. 256, 262, 265–66).

39. Cf., for example, Petty (1963, pp. 21, 157–58, 551ff.).

40. The existence of a natural demographic equilibrium linked to the level of technology had been suggested by Botero in *Della ragione di Stato* (1583, an English translation was published in 1606) and the idea will be given a central role by Malthus in his celebrated *Essay on the Principle of Population* (the first edition dates from 1798). In some passages of his writings Petty bases his calculations on the hypothesis of a geometric rate of growth of the population, anticipating one of the central hypotheses of the Malthusian theory (see, for example, *Another Essay in Political Arithmetick*, 1682, in Petty, 1963, pp. 451–78).

41. H. Lansdowne (1927, p. xxxvii).

42. Petty (1927, p. 208).

43. Cf. *Political Arithmetick* (1963, pp. 286–88).

44. Cf., for example, the *Two Essays in Political Arithmetick* (1963, pp. 504ff.).

45. Cf. *Another Essay in Political Arithmetick* (1963, pp. 470–71). Among the various advantages is also the prevention of civil uprisings, but elsewhere (1963, p. 40) Petty suggests that the existence of large cities represents a danger for the monarchy.

46. Petty (1963, pp. 475–76).

47. On the historical position and the diffusion of the opinion favorable to the increase in population in the seventeenth century cf. J. Schumpeter (1967, pp. 251–52).

Chapter 7

1. Cf. P. Sraffa (1960).
2. *A Treatise of Taxes and Contributions* (1963, p. 43). This passage is quoted by Marx (1969, p. 357), cf. also Marx (1962, p. 765). On the rate of interest, see chapter 3, section 5.
3. P. Sraffa (1960, pp. 113–14).
4. *A Treatise of Taxes and Contributions* (1963, p. 43). Exchange ratios will be discussed in chapter 8.
5. Ibid., p. 70.
6. See the passages referred to in notes 33, 34, and 35 in chapter 5, in particular, Petty (1963, pp. 30–31).
7. K. Marx (1969, p. 357).
8. See chapter 3, section 5.
9. Petty (1927a, p. 236).
10. Cf. chapter 5, section 5, and the passages referred to in notes 33, 34, and 35 of chapter 5. In terms of the reduction of the number of unproductive laborers, recall Petty's suggestion for the reduction of the general expenditures for the administration and the defense of the country (cf. chapter 6, section 5).
11. Cf., for example, *Political Arithmetick* (1963, pp. 256–57).
12. Ibid., pp. 249–50. The problem is mentioned throughout *Political Arithmetick*; see, for example, pp. 302–3.
13. "Bad Land may be improved and made good. . . ." Ibid., p. 249; see also pp. 302–3.
14. "One Man with a Mill can grind as much Corn, as twenty can pound in a Mortar; one Printer can make as many Copies, as a Hundred Men can write by hand. . . " Ibid., p. 249. Petty repeatedly affirms the importance of scientific research, from his first writings (Petty, 1648), to those of maturity (*Verbum Sapienti*, 1963, pp. 118–19).
15. *Political Arithmetick* (1963, pp. 260–61), see also Petty (1927a, p. 236).
16. *Another Essay in Political Arithmetick concerning the Growth of the City of London* (1963, p. 473).
17. J. Schumpeter (1967, p. 56). The importance of Plato as a precursor of Smith in the formulation of the division of labor has been recently emphasized by V. Foley (1974, pp. 220–42), even if substantial differences remain, as McNulty (1975, pp. 372–78) notes.
18. K. Marx (1970, pp. 365–67).
19. In terms of the territorial division of labor, recall Petty's recurrent proposal for *transplantation* of the Irish population, which was to leave Ireland as one large cattle farm (see chapter 6, note 38).
20. K. Marx (1970, pp. 364–65, italics added). Even if only incidentally, Petty does, in fact, recognize qualitative improvements: "when all the operations . . . were *clumsily* performed by the same hand"; "the watch will be *better* and cheaper," but there can be little doubt that there is a shift in emphasis, from the qualitative aspect to the quantitative aspect of the reduction in costs, with respect to the tradition of writers of Classical philosophy.
21. *Considerations on the East-India Trade* appeared in 1701 and was reprinted in McCulloch (1953, pp. 541–629). The passages relating to the division of labor can be found on pp. 590–92 of this edition.
22. Cf. Adam Smith (1976, pp. 14–15), and the entry *Epingle* in volume 5 of Diderot and d'Alembert's *Encyclopédie*, published between 1751 and 1772 (volume 5

dates from 1755). The example had already been used in the publicity brochure for the enterprise, see the *"Discours préliminaire"* by d'Alembert, published in 1751, although under the heading of "aiguille" (needle), rather than "épingle" (pin) (Diderot and d'Alembert, 1968, pp. 102–3). On the other hand, it is not clear that Smith had a sufficiently good knowledge of Petty's works, which do not appear in the lists of the contents of his personal library. Cf. Groenewegen (1968, p. 503).

23. Consider Marx's caustic judgment: "Adam Smith has not established a single new proposition relating to division of labour" (1970, p. 348n). Schumpeter's judgment is more general, and thus even more severe (although undoubtedly too drastic): "The *Wealth of Nations* does not contain a single *analytical* idea, principle or method that was entirely new in 1776" (1967, p. 184).

24. On Marx's ideas concerning the division of labor see in particular (1970) chapter XIV "Division of Labour and Manufacture" and chapter XV "Machinery and Modern Industry." For the reference to Petty's watch example see p. 342. The passage from *Political Arithmetick*, on the other hand, is cited by Marx in (1969, p. 180).

25. For example, Petty points out that "custom hath now made necessary to all sorts of people . . . Sugar, Tobacco and Pepper" *Political Arithmetick* (1963, p. 275).

26. *A Treatise of Taxes and Contributions* (1963, p. 52).

27. Cf., for example, Ricardo (1951, pp. 93–109).

28. T. Mun (1953, p. 182).

29. *A Treatise of Taxes and Contributions* (1963, p. 87).

30. That is, Petty suggests the hypothesis of negative (unitary) elasticity of the supply of labor with respect to wages. Cf., for example, *Political Arithmetick* (1963, pp. 274–75). At the beginning of the nineteenth century Malthus and Ricardo both agreed that such a hypothesis was valid in the case of the Spanish colonies in America and in Ireland. Cf. T. R. Malthus (1964, pp. 335–51) and D. Ricardo (1951a, pp. 336–37). The question had been discussed by letter between the two. In reply to Malthus, who had described the situation in Ireland, Ricardo suggests the comparison with the Spanish colonies, cf. Malthus' letter of August 17, 1817, and Ricardo's reply of September 4, 1817, (Ricardo, 1952a, pp. 174–76 and pp. 184–87 respectively). Smith, however, has an opinion just the opposite of Petty's: "The liberal reward of labour, therefore, as it is the effect of increasing wealth, so it is the cause of increasing population" (Smith, 1976, p. 99).

31. In the passage quoted above, Mun speaks of the "happiness of the people," in which he includes the "poor." He then continues "Whereby the burden (if any be) is still upon the rich, who are either idle, or at least work not in this kind, yet have they the use and are the great consumers of the poors labour" Mun (1953, p. 182). Mun was a rich director of the East-India company. It is more probable that his position reflects a tradition of medieval piety rather than a progressive pro-labor ideology, as improbable as that would have been at the time.

32. *Verbum Sapienti* (1963, p. 114).

33. *Political Arithmetick* (1963, p. 244).

34. *The Political Anatomy of Ireland* (1963, p. 194).

35. *A Treatise of Taxes and Contributions* (1963, p. 89).

36. Ibid., p. 48; cf. also pp. 51ff. The relation between the rate of interest, rent and the value of land has been discussed in chapter 3, section 5.

37. Cf. D. Ricardo (1951, pp. 70–71).

38. *A Treatise of Taxes and Contributions* (1963, p. 37).

39. Cf. Petty (1927, paper no. 62: "An Explication of Trade and Its Increase," pp. 210–14). The passage cited is on p. 214.

40. Cf., for example, *Political Arithmetick* (1963, pp. 289–90).

41. We have already seen in chapter 6, section 6, that the differences in the growth potential of the various sectors translates into a scale of profitability in which the

traditional sectors, such as agriculture, occupy the lower rungs; it is this fact that explains the low wages of agricultural workers relative to other sectors (which has, however, the effect of preventing a reduction in rents: cf. *Political Arithmetick*, 1963, pp. 267–68).

Chapter 8

1. *The Dialogue of Diamonds* (1963, pp. 624–30).
2. "I am afrayed I gave too much for it, & the truth is I wonder how any man (can) tell what to give, there be so many nice considerations in that matter in all which one has nothing but meere guesse to guide himself by" (Ibid., pp. 624–25).
3. "I had shewed it to 2 or 3 friends, who all, to shew their skill, made some special animadversions upon the business & told me I could not be much out if I gave between 80 & 90 £., for it" (Ibid., p. 626).
4. "In the economic field . . . there was a period in which 'science' could not exist, not only because there were no scientists, but because the preconditions which create those particular 'regularities' or 'automatisms' whose study provides the origin of scientific research were not present," A. Gramsci (1975, p. 1350), see also p. 1477–79.
5. *The Dialogue of Diamonds* (1963, p. 627). This rule, together with the others of a similar nature, were also proposed by Petty in his *Discourse Concerning the Use of Duplicate Proportion*, published in 1674 (and reprinted in part in Petty, 1963, pp. 622–23) where he attempts the expression of pairs of variables in functional terms on the condition that there is sufficient regularity in the relationship between the phenomena considered and that they can be expressed in quantitative terms. This attempt places Petty at the head of the precursors, or perhaps among the founders, of econometrics.
6. *The Dialogue of Diamonds* (1963, pp. 627–28).
7. Ibid., pp. 626–27. For example, Mr. A suggests for the case of defects: "you must have as many foule diamonds as doe contein Samples of every sort of fault & a note of such abatements as an experienced Jeweller would make for every such fault, the same to be expressed in aliquot parts of the whole value" (Ibid., p. 627).
8. Ibid., p. 630.
9. A typical example of the definition of a commodity on the basis of the level of abstraction implicit in a particular analytical framework is offered to us by Petty who identifies "wheat" with "food" in general when (in *A Treatise of Taxes and Contributions*, 1963, p. 89) he speaks of "Corn, which we will suppose to contain all necessaries for life, as in the Lords Prayer we suppose the word Bread doth." This identification is adopted implicitly by Ricardo (*An Essay on the Influence of a Low Price of Corn on the Profits of Stock*, in D. Ricardo, 1951b, pp. 1–42) who was quickly criticized by Malthus (letter to Ricardo dated March 12, 1815, in ibid., 1952, p. 185). More recently, Petty's hypothesis has been explicitly referred to by A. Marshall (1961, p. 509, note 2) and by P. Sraffa (1925, p. 324, note 1).
10. *A Treatise of Taxes and Contributions* (1963, p. 90).
11. The analogy concerns the technology to which reference should be made. Both Petty's "political price" and the "natural price" of the Classics are based on that currently existing, that is, on the prevailing technology and not on the optimal technology which, as noted above, seems to be more closely associated with Petty's "natural price." But, for the Classical economists and for Marx there is an automatic mechanism, competition, that eliminates wastes and tends to adjust the prevailing technology to the optimal. For Petty, on the other hand (and understandably, given the period in which he lived), such a role is attributed to intervention by means of institutional

engineering meant to make the operation of the system more efficient.

12. Ibid., p. 90.

13. *The Dialogue of Diamonds* (1963, p. 625).

14. Cf., for example, *Political Arithmetick* (1963, pp. 298–302) where various institutional factors are included among the "contingent and removable impediments" to the development of England's wealth. See also, chapter 6, section 5.

15. Such as that adopted, for example, by Adam Smith (1976, pp. 72–81, Book I, chapter VII, "Of the natural and market Price of Commodities") or by David Ricardo (1951, pp. 88–92, chapter IV, "On Natural and Market Price").

16. Cf., for example, Marx (1969, pp. 181–82), H. Denis (1973, p. 172), R. Meek (1973, pp. 34–36), G. Pietranera (1963, pp. 31–50), and E. Roll (1956, pp. 100–11).

17. *A Treatise of Taxes and Contributions* (1963, p. 43).

18. Ibid., p. 80. Cf. also the passages from *A Dialogue on Political Arithmetick* quoted in chapter 6, note 2 where Petty appears to be using the typically Marxian notions of "necessary" and "surplus" labor.

19. Petty (1963, p. 44). See also *A Dialogue on Political Arithmetick* (reprinted in Matsukawa, 1977, p. 47) where Petty tackles the problem of the "Par between lands and hands" (and resolves it by reference to "Money (which) is the Common denominator by which the Par is made," i.e., relying on the money values of rents and wages as given data of the problem), while referring in the same context to the labor contained in gold and silver as the factor determining their relative price.

20. The reader should be aware that Marx's conception of the theory of value and that associated with the Classical economists are not generally considered to be identical. On the argument, see L. Colletti (1968).

21. *A Treatise of Taxes and Contributions* (1963, p. 68).

22. R. Tawney (1975, p. 48) after having described such a theory, is led to state (erroneously) that "The true descendant of the doctrines of Aquinas is the labour theory of value. The last of the Schoolmen was Karl Marx."

23. Cf. *The Holy Bible*, Genesis, 3:14–19. After the original sin "The Lord . . . said to man: . . . In the sweat of thy face shalt thou eat bread."

24. Elements of such a conception are also present at various places in Smith who considered labor as "toil and trouble." It is taken up and developed by Marshall in his concept of "real costs."

25. See chapter 7, section 4 and the passage from *The Political Anatomy of Ireland* (1963, p. 181) cited in the subsequent section.

26. *The Political Anatomy of Ireland* (1963, p. 181). The same problem is also considered in *A Treatise of Taxes and Contributions* (1963, p. 44).

27. In particular, Petty never considers the problem of the "original source of wealth" in the same sense in which it would be subsequently confronted by the Physiocrats. The ranking of the "productivity" of the various sectors is based on relative profitability or on the "durability" of the respective outputs (see chapter 6, section 6 on the question).

28. Petty (1927, p. 190). Petty in fact conceives of prices as being determined by relative difficulties of production of the various commodities: "when the difficultyes (of production) change then Prices change also," *A Dialogue on Political Arithmetick* (reprinted in Matsukawa, 1977, p. 47). He summarized these "difficulties" in a single magnitude (labor), or in two magnitudes (labor and land), or described them fully by means of a complete list of the required means of production.

29. Petty (1927, p. 190).

30. To be precise, it should be noted that physical costs are not a purely technological category. This is not only because their magnitude (especially in the case of labor) depends on social factors in a general sense, but also because the inputs which are included in costs depend on the method of social organization. For example, only those

factors that can be privately appropriated are included as inputs under capitalism (but not rain, or the sun, which are necessary to production and which may be considered as scarce).

31. *The Political Anatomy of Ireland* (1963, p. 181). The symbol C. represents a hundredweight, or 112 pounds in English usage. This passage has also been interpreted (for example by G. Routh, 1975, p. 40) as an example of marginal calculation: the "contribution" of each "productive factor" is obtained by calculating what would be obtained by using the factor in isolation from the other, or by increasing the quantity of the factor employed, holding constant the quantity of the other factor. The objection raised earlier in this chapter concerning the problem arising from the existence of heterogeneous factors also applies to this interpretation. The heterogeneous factors could only be reduced to homogeneous quantities—in terms of utility—within the context of a fully subjective theory of value.

32. *The Political Anatomy of Ireland* (1963, p. 181). See also the passage from *A Treatise of Taxes and Contributions* (1963, p. 89) already referred to in note 9 above, where Petty speaks of "Corn, which we will suppose to contain all necessaries for life, as in the Lords Prayer we suppose the word Bread doth."

33. *The Political Anatomy of Ireland* (1963, p. 182). The same proposal is applied by Petty to other factors: "By the same way also an Equation may be made between drudging Labour, and Favour, Acquaintance, Interest, Friends, Eloquence, Reputation, Power, Authority, &c."

34. R. Cantillon (1931, p. 22).

35. Ibid., p. 30.

36. Ibid., p. 26.

37. Ibid., p. 25–26.

38. *The Political Anatomy of Ireland* (Petty, 1963, p. 181).

39. See F. Quesnay (1958) and M. Ridolfi (1973).

40. "In every society the price of every commodity finally resolves itself into some one or other, or all of those three parts (namely wages, profits and rent), and in every improved society all the three enter more or less, as component parts, into the price of the far greater part of commodities" (A. Smith, 1976, p. 68. The argument is developed in chapter VI of Book I "Of the Component Parts of the Price Commodities," pp. 65–71).

41. P. Sraffa (1951, p. xxxv).

42. On Smith's theory of prices, and Ricardo's criticisms, cf. P. Sraffa (1951, pp. xxxiii ff.) and M. Dobb (1973).

43. In his *A Treatise of Taxes and Contributions* Petty also refers to the conditions of equality of profitability in the various sectors, stating that two laborers employed for the same time, one in the production of wheat, the other in the production of silver, should produce a surplus of equal value. However, the uniformity of profitability should be considered with reference to capital advanced and not, as in Petty's argument, to labor expended. A number of pre-Smithian economists also recognized the point (see in particular, R.J. Turgot, 1973,) although the uniformity of the rate of profit in the various sectors was not a crucial aspect of their analyses.

44. D. Ricardo (1951b, pp. 9–41).

45. See, for example, the letters of August 5, 1814, and of March 12 and 14, 1815, in Ricardo (1952, pp. 117–18 and 185–87). R. Torrens should also be mentioned in this context (1821). He distinguished two commodities each of which, in reality, was an aggregate of heterogeneous goods: the output of the industrial sector and the output of the agricultural sector. Both of the commodities are necessary as inputs in their own production and in the production of the other good, as either means of production or subsistence goods.

46. See. D. Ricardo (1951).

47. On the pre-Ricardian and the pre-Smithian labor theories of value see R. Meek (1973, pp. 11–42).

48. Among the numerous essays treating this question the reader is referred to that of S. Vicarelli (1975) which conscientiously reviews each relevant stage of the debate in connection with Marx's interpretation of the theory of value.

49. P. Sraffa (1960).

Chapter 9

1. In a letter to Keynes dated April 9, 1937, Hicks declares that he has "made a practice of restraining my interest in the history of theory at 1870" (quoted in Keynes, 1973, p. 81). The statement is indicative, although in recent years Hicks himself has not followed his own advice.

2. K. Marx (1951).

3. K. Marx (1969, pp. 180–82, 354–64).

4. See chapter 8, section 4.

5. J. Cartelier (1976, p. 18).

6. We will only call attention to one case which seems of particular current relevance. Neither in Classical political economy, or in the modern variety, is it possible to find a discussion of the concept of market or of commodity similar to that offered by Petty in *The Dialogue of Diamonds*. Having acquired a sort of scientific status dignity these concepts are accepted and utilized without further discussion. When their content is modified in order to allow their utilization in a particular analytical framework, the fact that the same name is used to describe what is, in fact, a new analytical concept tends to obscure the change in the theoretical point of view and creates a fictitious continuity between the old and the new analytical frameworks. For example, when one discovers that the concept of price employed by the modern marginal theory is not the same as that used by the Classical economists, it is opportune to reread the works of those authors, such as Petty, who explicitly discuss such problems.

Bibliography

Ashley, M. (1970) *England in the Seventeenth Century*, 3rd ed. Harmondsworth: Penguin.

Aubrey, J. (1813) "Brief Lives," in *Bodleian Letters*, eds. Walker and Bliss. Vol. II. Oxford.

Bacon, F. (1968) *Novum Organum, I. Aforismi sull'interpretazione della natura*, trans. E. De Mas. Bari: Laterza.

Bacon, F. (1965) *The Advancement of Learning*. London: Dent, Everyman's Library.

Barbon, N. (1690) *Discourse of Trade*. Reprint edited by J. H. Hollander. Baltimore: Johns Hopkins Press, 1934.

Bevan, W. L. (1894) "Sir William Petty: A Study in English Economic Literature," in *Publications of the American Economic Association*. Vol. IX, no. 4, pp. 370–472.

Böhm-Bawerk, E. (1890) *Capital and Interest*, trans. W. Smart. London: Macmillan.

Bora, P. (1980) "Sir William Petty: macchina e organismo alle origini dell'economia politica," in *Transactions of the Fifth International Congress on the Enlightenment*, ed. by H. Mason. The Voltaire Foundation, Oxford, pp. 804–11.

Botero, G. (1583) *Della ragione di Stato*. Venezia (4th ed. Turin: Gio. Domenico Tarino, 1596).

Bowley, M. (1963) *Studies in the History of Economic Thought Before 1870*. London: Macmillan.

Cannan, E. (1964) *A Review of Economic Theory*, 2nd ed. London: F. Cass.

Cantillon, R. (1931) *Essai sur la Nature du Commerce en Général*, edited and translated in English by H. Higgs. London: F. Cass.

Capitani, P. (1975) "Introduzione" to *La nascita dell'economia politica*. Turin: Loescher.

Carsten, F. (1969) "The Ascendancy of France," in *The New Cambridge Modern History*, Vol. V. Cambridge: Cambridge University Press.

Cartelier, J. (1976) *Surproduit et Reproduction*. Grenoble: Presses Universitaires de Grenoble and Maspero.

Cerroni, U. (1973) "W. Petty fondatore della teoria del valore-lavoro," *Politica ed economia*. Vol. IV, no. 5, pp. 96–100.

Child, J. (1690) *A Discourse about Trade, wherein the Reduction of Interest of Money to 4l. per Centum, is recommended. . . .* London.

Coats, A. (1975) "Adam Smith and the Mercantile System," in *Essays on Adam* eds. A. Skinner and T. Wilson. Oxford: Clarendon Press.

Colletti, L. (1968) "Introduzione" to E. Bernstein, *I presupposti del socialismo e i compiti della socialdemocrazia*. Bari: Laterza.

Denis, H. (1973) *Storia del pensiero economico*, trans. F. Rodano. Milan: Mondadori.

Diderot, D. and d'Alembert, J. B. (1968) *Enciclopedia*, selections edited by P. Casini. Bari: Laterza.

Dobb, M. (1973) "Introduzione" to A. Smith, *Indagine sulla natura e le cause della ricchezza delle nazioni*, trans F. Bartoli, C. Camporesi, S. Caruso. Milan: ISEDI.

Dobb, M. (1973) *Theories of value and distribution since Adam Smith*. Cambridge: Cambridge University Press.

Dusenberry, J. (1949) *Income, Saving, and the Theory of Consumer Behavior*. Cambridge, Mass.: Harvard University Press.

Einaudi, L. (1932) "Di un quesito intorno alla nascita della scienza economica," *Riforma Sociale*. March-April, pp. 219–25.

Einaudi, L. (1941) *Saggi sul risparmio e l'imposta*. Turin: Einaudi.

Engels, F. (1962) *Anti-Dühring*. Moscow: Foreign Languages Publishing House.

Fitzmaurice, E. (1895) *The Life of Sir William Petty*. London: Murray.

Foley, V. (1974) "The Division of Labor in Plato and Smith," *History of Political Economy*. Vol. VI, pp. 220–42.

Galilei, G. (1890–1909) *Il Saggiatore* (1623), in *Le opere*. Vol. VI, ed. A. Favaro. Florence.

Gramsci, A. (1968) *Lettere dal carcere*, eds. S. Caprioglio and E. Fubini. Turin: Einaudi.

Gramsci, A. (1975) *Quaderni del carcere*, ed. V. Gerratana. Turin: Einaudi. Partially translated in *Prison Notebooks*, eds. Q. Hoare and G. Nowell Smith. London: Lawrence and Wishart, 1971.

Groenewegen, P. D. (1967) "Authorship of the *Natural and Political Observations Upon the Bills of Mortality*," *Journal of the History of Ideas*. Vol. XXVIII, no. 4, Oct.-Dec., pp. 601-2.

Groenewegen, P. D. (1968) "A New Catalogue of Adam Smith's Library," *Economic Record*. Vol. XLIV, Dec., pp. 498-506.

Groenewegen, P. D. (1971) "A Re-interpretation of Turgot's Theory of Captial and Interest," *Economic Journal*. Vol. LXXXI, pp. 327-40.

Hicks, J. R. (1983) "The Social Accounting of Classical Models," in *Classics and Moderns: Collected Essays on Economic Theory*. Vol. III. Oxford: Blackwell.

Higgs, H. (1895) "Review of W. L. Bevan, 'Sir William Petty. A Study in English Economic Literature,' " *Economic Journal*. Vol. V, pp. 71-72.

Higgs, H. (1895a) "Review of H. Fitzmaurice, 'The Life of Sir William Petty,' " *Economic Journal*. Vol. V, pp. 251-52.

Hill, C. (1972) *Intellectual Origins of the English Revolution*, 3rd ed. London: Panther.

Hobbes, T. (1946) *Leviathan*. Oxford: Blackwell.

Holtrop, M. (1928) *De Omloopsnelheid van het Geld*. Amsterdam.

Holtrop, M. (1929) "Theories of the Velocity of Circulation of Money in Earlier Economic Literature," *Economic History*.

Hull, C. (1895) "Review of W. L. Bevan, 'Sir William Petty. A Study in English Economic Literature,' " *Political Science Quarterly*. Vol. X, pp. 334-38.

Hull, C. (1900) "Petty's Place in the History of Economic Theory," *Quarterly Journal of Economics*. Vol. XIV, pp. 307-40.

Hull, C. (1963) "Introduction" to W. Petty, *Economic Writings of Sir William Petty*, two vols. (1899). New York: A. Kelley.

Johnson, E. A. G. (1937) *Precursors of Adam Smith*. London: P. S. King.

Kaldor, N. (1955) *An Expenditure Tax*. London: Allen and Unwin.

Keynes, G. (1971) *A Bibliography of Sir William Petty, F.R.S. and of Observations on the Bills of Mortality by John Graunt, F.R.S.* Oxford: Clarendon Press.

Keynes, J. M. (1936) *The General Theory of Employment, Interest and Money*. London: Macmillan.

Keynes, J. M. (1973) *The General Theory and After. Defence and Development*. Vol. XIV of *The Collected Writings of John Maynard Keynes*. London: Macmillan for the Royal Economic Society.

Lansdowne, H. (1927) "Introduction" to W. Petty, *Papers*, two vols. London: Constable.

Letwin, W. (1956) "Review of E. Strauss, *Sir William Petty: Portrait of a Genius*," *Journal of Political Economy*. Vol. LXIV, p. 180.

Letwin, W. (1963) *The Origins of Scientific Economics. English Economic Thought, 1660-1776*. London: Methuen.

Locke, J. (1691) *Some Considerations on the Consequences of the Lowering of Interest, and Raising the Value of Money*. London.

Malthus, T. R. (1798) *An Essay on the Principle of Population*. New York: Macmillan Co. Reprint, 1909.

Malthus, T. R. (1964) *Principles of Political Economy*, 2nd ed. New York: A. M. Kelley.

Marshall, A. (1961) *Principles of Economics*, 9th, Variorum edition, ed. C. Guillebaud. London: Macmillan.

Marshall, A. (1923) *Money, Credit and Commerce*. London: Macmillan.

Marx, K. (1941) "Theses on Feuerbach," appendix to F. Engels, *Ludwig Feuerbach and the Outcome of Classical German Philosophy*. New York: International Publishers.

Marx, K. (1951) *Theories of Surplus Value*, ed. K. Kautsky, trans. E. Bonner and E. Burns. London: Lawrence and Wishart.

Marx, K. (1962) *Capital*. Vol. III. Moscow: Foreign Languages Publishing House.

Marx, K. (1969) *Theories of Surplus Value*. Vol. I. London: Lawrence and Wishart.

Marx, K. (1970) *Capital*. Vol. I. London: Lawrence and Wishart.

Marx, K. (1971) *A Contribution to the Critique of Political Economy*. London: Lawrence and Wishart.

Marx, K. (1973) *Grundrisse*, trans. M. Nicolaus. London: Penguin.

Marx, K. (no date) *The Poverty of Philosophy*. Chicago: Kerr.

Matsukawa, S. (1955) "Origin and Significance of Political Arithmetick," *The Annals of the Hitotsubashi Academy*. Vol. II, pp. 53-79.

Matsukawa, S. (1965) "An Essay on the Historical Uniqueness of Petty's Labour Theory of Value," *Hitotsubashi Journal of Economics*. Vol. V, pp. 1-11.

Matsukawa, S. (1977) "Sir William Petty: An Unpublished Manuscript," *Hitotsubashi Journal of Economics*. Vol. XVII, no. 2, pp. 33-50.

McCulloch, J. (1953) *Early English Tracts on Commerce* (1856). Cambridge: Economic History Society Reprint.

McCulloch, J. (1953a) *Scarce and Valuable Tracts on Money* (1856). Cambridge: Economic History Society Reprint.

McNulty, P. (1975) "A Note on the Division of Labor in Plato and Smith," *History of Political Economy*. Vol. VII, pp. 372-78.

Meek, R. (1973) *Studies in the Labour Theory of Value*, 2nd ed. London: Lawrence and Wishart.

Muller, W. (1932) *William Petty als Politischer Arithmetiker: Eine Soziologisch-statistische Studie*. Gelnhausen.

Mun, T. (1953) *England's Treasure by Forraign Trade*, in J. McCulloch, *Early English Tracts on Commerce*. Op. cit., pp. 115-209.

Okun, A. (1962) "Potential G.N.P.: Its Measurement and Significance," *Papers and Proceedings of the American Statistical Association*.

Pasquier, M. (1903) *Sir William Petty. Ses Idées Economiques*. Paris: Giard et Brière.

Petty, W. (1648) *Advice of W.P. to Mr. Samuel Hartlib*. London.

Petty, W. (1905) *Oeuvres économiques*, trans. H. Dussauze and M. Pasquier. Paris: Giard et Brière.

Petty, W. (1927) *Papers*. Vol. I, ed. H. Lansdowne. London: Constable.

Petty, W. (1927a) *Papers*. Vol. II, ed. H. Lansdowne. London: Constable.

Petty, W. (1928) *Petty-Southwell Correspondence 1676-1687*, ed. H. Lansdowne. London: Constable.

Petty, W. (1963) *Economic Writings of Sir William Petty*, ed. C. Hull (1899), two vols. New York: A. M. Kelley.

Petty, W. (1972) *Scritti*, ed. P. Colussi. Milan: Iota Libri.

Pietranera, G. (1963) *La teoria del valore e dello sviluppo capitalistico in Adamo Smith*. Milan: Feltrinelli.

Potter, W. (1650) *The Key of Wealth*. London.

Pufendorf, S. (1934) *De Jure Naturae et Gentium libri octo*, trans. C. and W. Oldfather, in the *The Classics of International Law*. No. 17, Vol. II. Oxford: Clarendon Press.

Quesnay, F. (1765) "Observations sur le droit naturel des hommes réunis en société," *Journal de l'agriculture, du commerce et des finances*. Vol. 2, September.

Quesnay, F. (1958) *Francois Quesnay et la Fisiocratie*. Paris: INED.

Ricardo, D. (1951) *The Principles of Political Economy and Taxation*. Vol. I of *The Works and Correspondence of D. Ricardo*, ed. P. Sraffa with M. Dobb. Cambridge: Cambridge University Press.

Ricardo, D. (1951a) *Notes on Malthus*, in Vol. II of *The Works and Correspondence of D. Ricardo*. Op. cit.

Ricardo, D. (1951b) *Pamphlets and Papers 1815-1823*. Vol. IV of *The Works and Correspondence of D. Ricardo*. Op.cit.

Ricardo, D. (1952) *Letters 1810-1815*. Vol. VI of *The Works and Correspondence of D. Ricardo*. Op. cit.

Ricardo, D. (1952a) *Letters 1816-1818*. Vol. VII of *The Works and Correspondence of D. Ricardo*. Op. cit.

Ridolfi, M. (1973) "Introduzione" to F. Quesnay, *Il Tableau Economique e altri scritti di economia*. Milan: ISEDI.

Roll, E. (1956) *History of Economic Thought*, 3rd ed. Englewood Cliffs, N.J.: Prentice-Hall.

Routh, G. (1975) *The Origins of Economic Ideas*. London: Macmillan.

Schumpeter, J. (1967) *History of Economic Analysis*, 6th ed. London: Allen and Unwin.

Selden, R.T. (1956) "Monetary Velocity in the United States," in M. Friedman, ed., *Stud-

ies in the Quantity Theory of Money. Chicago: University of Chicago Press.

Smith, A. (1976) *An Inquiry into the Nature and Causes of the Wealth of Nations*, eds., R. Campbell, A. Skinner, and W. Todd. Oxford: Clarendon Press (Glasgow Edition).

Sraffa, P. (1925) "Sulle relazioni fra costo e quantità prodotta," *Annali di Economia*. Vol. II, pp. 277–328.

Sraffa, P. (1951) "Introduction" to D. Ricardo, *The Works and Correspondence of D. Ricardo*. Op. cit., pp. xiii-lxii.

Sraffa, P. (1960) *Production of Commodities By Means of Commodities*. Cambridge: Cambridge University Press.

Strauss, E. (1954) *Sir William Petty. Portrait of a Genius*. London: The Bodley Head.

Tawney, R. (1975) *Religion and the Rise of Capitalism* (1926). Harmondsworth: Penguin.

Torrens, R. (1821) *Essay on the Production of Wealth*. London.

Tucker, G. (1960) *Progress and Profits in British Economic Thought 1650-1850*. Cambridge: Cambridge University Press.

Turgot, R. J. (1973) *Reflections on the Formation and the Distribution of Wealth*, in *Turgot on Progress, Sociology and Economics*, ed. and trans. R. Meek. Cambridge: Cambridge University Press.

Vicarelli, S. (1975) "Il problema della trasformazione: fine di una controversia?" *Note economiche*. Vol. VIII, pp. 91–138.

Viner, J. (1964) *Studies in the Theory of International Trade*, 4th ed. London: Allen and Unwin.

DATE DUE
